CED

D1510777

THE BIKER
WHO SHOT ME

ALSO BY MICHEL AUGER

The Heroin Triangle (1978)

THE BIKER
WHO SHOT ME

Recollections of a Crime Reporter

Michel Auger

Translated by Jean-Paul Murray

M&S

Original French-language edition © 2001
Éditions trait d'union and Michel Auger
English translation © 2002 McClelland & Stewart Ltd. and Jean-Paul Murray

National Library of Canada Cataloguing in Publication Data

Auger, Michel, 1944-
The biker who shot me: recollections of a crime reporter /
Michel Auger ; translated by Jean-Paul Murray.

Traduction de : L'attentat.
ISBN 0-7710-0877-5

1. Auger, Michel, 1944-.   2. Organized crime investigation – Quebec
(Province)   3. Organized crime.   4. Victims of crimes – Quebec (Province)
– Montréal – Biography.   5. Journalists – Quebec (Province) – Montréal
– Biography.   I. Murray, Jean-Paul, 1960-   II. Title.

HV6439.C32Q814 2002a   362.88´092   C2002-901446-8

We acknowledge the financial support of the Government of Canada through
the Book Publishing Industry Development Program for our publishing
activities. We further acknowledge the support of the Canada Council for the
Arts and the Ontario Arts Council for our publishing program.

The translation of this book was assisted by a grant
from the Government of Québec (SODEC).

Published simultaneously in the United States of America by
McClelland & Stewart Ltd., P.O. Box 1030, Plattsburgh, New York 12901

Library of Congress Control Number: 2002104568

Typeset in Plantin by M&S, Toronto
Printed and bound in Canada

McClelland & Stewart Ltd.
The Canadian Publishers
481 University Avenue
Toronto, Ontario
M5G 2E9
www.mcclelland.com

1 2 3 4 5   06 05 04 03 02

To my daughter, Guylaine,
to my grandson, Nicolas,
and to my granddaughter, Amélie

Contents

	Preface by Jean-Pierre Charbonneau	ix
1.	A Beautiful September Day	1
2.	My Start in Journalism	23
3.	The Cotronis	35
4.	Two Major Investigations	47
5.	Famous Criminals	57
6.	Strong Competition	87
7.	Television Moments	95
8.	Several Explosive Issues	115
9.	The Bikers in My Life	145
10.	A Lost Day	165
11.	Two Weeks to Ponder	177
12.	Tributes	187
13.	The Biker Who Became a Celebrity	197
14.	An Active Investigation	203
	By Way of Conclusion	213
	Acknowledgements	217

Preface

*T*he great Quebec journalist and statesman René Lévesque often said that there is no real freedom without information.

Informing the public adequately to help it understand, choose, and act is therefore an important task. It requires a near-obsessive curiosity, a special passion for knowledge and for gathering facts, as well as unequivocal commitment to truth and accuracy.

In this book, Michel Auger tells us how and why he became a journalist – a very good one, in my view – and, especially, how and why he gradually became the Quebec public's best source of information on the activities of our society's petty and major crooks.

This book isn't an exercise in self-gratification. It's the thrilling account of a career and of the events that allowed it to flourish to the point where Auger became, outside the underworld and the legal apparatus, an individual that mob barons fear and despise.

Uncovering the activities of professional criminals, and of the various organizations grouping them, isn't easy, for the plain and simple reason that they're illegal and clandestine.

To get a good grasp of the underworld and, particularly, to know precisely what goes on in it, journalists have few options. Associating *with the police goes hand in hand with doing their jobs correctly and efficiently. This angers criminals, who foolishly want journalists to remain impartial and, moreover, to say nothing about them or, at the very least, nothing offensive. What arrogance!*

They kill or have others killed; they rob or have others rob; they threaten and intimidate directly or get goons to do so; they abuse, exploit, corrupt our friends, parents, children, and, to top it all off, would prefer we remain quiet and leave them alone or portray them as heroes and "good guys."

Michel Auger has always refused to play along with mob bosses. He has sided with the public's right to know and understand. Accordingly, he has chosen to keep company with police officers, those who, paid with our taxes, are responsible for knowing what goes on in the underworld. They're the ones who prevent gangs from appropriating too much power in a society that sometimes takes the protection of rights to a ridiculous extent.

Naturally, Auger has chosen his camp by favouring police sources over criminal ones; however, this hasn't prevented him from maintaining his independence or integrity.

In the hours following the attempt on his life, some, including journalists, claimed that Auger was at fault since he didn't stick to reporting facts. He dared to establish links! Yet he'd only done his job, which requires – to be done adequately – that citizens understand the extent of certain hidden realities.

As a citizen and elected representative, I'm delighted by Michel Auger's work. His aggressive and dedicated investigative journalism has helped us avoid being lulled by reassuring statistics on crime. He reminds us regularly of the magnitude of underworld activity.

As a friend, I'm proud of him, proud that he taught me the profession of journalism. Thanks to him, I feel I did good work in the six years I practised the same type of journalism he does.

Moreover, I'm filled with admiration and tip my hat to him when I think he's been doing this job with efficiency and passion for thirty-seven years.

Jean-Pierre Charbonneau
journalist and representative
Minister of Intergovernmental Affairs, Quebec

| 1 |

A Beautiful September Day

In life, some days are so beautiful they make you feel as though you hover over everything and nothing can bother you. For me, September 13, 2000, was such a day. The sun was shining in Montreal. I was returning from a delightful holiday and expecting a stress-free work week. I was even thinking about the upcoming weekend I'd spend in the country with family and friends.

In the last few weeks, I had decided to get really serious about planning for my retirement in four or five years. I felt I should play a more low-key role. I would stop doing interviews with my radio and television colleagues who solicited me whenever events linked to organized crime disturbed the peace. I was hoping my face would be forgotten and that I could go about the town unrecognized.

Over the years, I had become a specialist of the underworld. The mob no longer had any secrets for me. I have a good memory and was able to provide background information whenever an attempted murder or an eruption of gang violence occurred. I had been familiar with the Canadian, American, and

Italian Mafias for a long time. But since 1995, the Hells Angels were what kept me the busiest. The motorcycle gang, created in the late 1940s in California by disenchanted Second World War veterans, had considerably evolved, and was now part of organized crime. They weren't only bikers, but also wealthy and ultra-sophisticated criminals at the leading edge of technology.

This was the stuff of my daily work. I liked the challenge. My professional satisfaction came from finding and revealing the activities of these people who live on the fringes of society. I was happy when I could show how these criminals, who felt they were above the law and smarter than honest workers, went about exploiting the public.

September 13, 2000, was indeed a beautiful and quiet day. I had planned to have lunch with a police officer who specialized in organized crime. He was easily bored by routine and constantly seeking new informers to get good leads. If I'd been a cop, I'd have wanted to be like him. In fact, during my childhood in Shawinigan, I'd thought about becoming a policeman or a fireman, but these were only dreams.

In those days Shawinigan was called the city of electricity. Few of its residents then would have guessed that, a few years later, its population, about fifty thousand at the time, would decrease by half. Its most famous son, Jean Chrétien, would have a long political career before becoming prime minister of Canada. Just like him, other young people from the area would seek work elsewhere, many of them in Montreal, a great city for a young man, filled with action, entertainment, and, especially, jobs.

I had no idea what direction my life would take, but a casual job would open my eyes. I experienced the atmosphere of a newsroom at the age of nineteen and discovered that the job of reporter was wonderful. I was bewitched by this world where nothing is ever foreseen, where cranks rub shoulders with intellectuals, where individuals from every walk of life and widely divergent political views are bound together by the same obsession: the news.

I had become a journalist covering a beat looked down upon by many of my colleagues in the media: the news-in-brief, which is the page dealing with minor news items.

Routine journalism has never been my strong point. I have always liked a challenge. But the big issues, the great journalistic investigations, don't unfold in the offices of newspapers or radio and television stations. Good clues are found on the street. It's true that people do call us to denounce a scandal, to give us valuable leads, but most informers provide useless information, and quality tips are the exception. It's left to journalists to make the difference by being able to identify hot issues and items that will make a splash amid the stream of rumours and seemingly trivial developments.

This is my style of journalism.

Place Versailles is a shopping centre in Montreal's east end. It includes an office tower that houses the Montreal Urban Community's (MUC) specialized police squads. This is where investigators dealing with drugs, fraud, bank robberies, and murders ply their trade. It also houses experts in criminal intelligence who sift through files, exploring all avenues to help detectives in the line of fire. The anti-gang squad also has an operations centre on Sherbrooke Street East.

I often repaired to the offices of these specialized squads, where I would meet senior officers who oversee files, as well as regular constables and non-commissioned officers who gather evidence that will eventually be submitted to a judge. Place Versailles is also where, over the last several months, I had often run into the Hells Angels' upper management. Maurice "Mom" Boucher and his close colleagues had fallen into the habit of haunting the centre's restaurants to taunt police officers, as well as the *Journal de Montréal* reporter who occasionally frequented the huge building.

This popular morning daily is the preferred reading of bikers. Though the majority of *Journal de Montréal* readers are far from being criminals, gangsters are among its most loyal readers. That's why Mom and his pals often had comments and suggestions to make about my way of reporting the news. They would have preferred, for instance, to read fewer negative items on the biker war and on the role played by the Hells Angels. After all, weren't they entitled to a more positive image as officials of an organization bringing in billions of dollars to Quebec?

But the biker war started by the Hells Angels had claimed nearly 160 victims, including 17 completely innocent people – eleven-year-old Daniel Desrochers among them. Under the circumstances, positive publicity is not only difficult, it's impossible.

Boucher had always declined to give interviews, as had the other gang members I had approached. On a few occasions, some gang members, likely without mentioning it to their associates, agreed to discuss certain issues with me, on condition they never be identified. But for Boucher and his staff, in-depth conversations were out of the question. The public's right to complete information wasn't in the gang leaders' plans.

On the morning of September 13, I had an appointment with Det.-Lieut. Jean-François Martin, one of the homicide squad's two investigation coordinators who shares the supervision of fifty or so homicide investigations yearly with his colleague Stephen Roberts.

It seems that there are fewer murder victims in Quebec today, partly because doctors are able to save the lives of many people who are more or less seriously wounded. This is the kind of subject I would discuss with police officers now and again. The issue was topical because, less than twenty-four hours earlier, I had published a two-page article on the biker war and its victims, who, until then, had been reputedly untouchable, like certain individuals linked to the underworld and said to be on the best of terms with Mafia bigwigs. For his part, Martin was interested in the details of the death threats I had received the previous day during a phone conversation with the wife of François Gagnon. Gagnon, a petty criminal who weighed more than 160 kilograms, had been gunned down as a result of the biker war. Though not very involved in biker business, Gagnon, who loved to chat, would talk about his close friendship with Salvatore Cazetta, head of the Rock Machine, sworn enemies to the Hells Angels. That morning, I also had a conversation with the director of organized-crime investigations, Inspector Serge Frenette, who was in charge of the anti-gang squad conducting several investigations linked to the bloody biker feud. As usual, our conversations were punctuated by phone calls and other assorted interruptions.

In addition to the conversations with the police officers this morning, I had a telephone discussion with one of my bosses, Serge Labrosse, assistant to the news director in charge of court activities and of local news in particular. Since I had nothing specific in the works for the day, our conversation had been rather brief. I also confirmed with my daughter, Guylaine, that I'd babysit my grandson, Nicolas, in the evening. She and her husband, Carl Bourcier, were scheduled to visit the delivery room where she was to give birth to her second child, Amélie, one month later.

I remember the lovely weather that day and how motorists and people in general seemed relaxed. Life was good. There are days when the pedestrians you pass in the street seem bellicose or nervous, but this was definitely not the case this morning.

Only a few minutes are needed by car to get from the police station to the *Journal de Montréal*'s offices on Frontenac Street, at the juncture of the Hochelaga-Maisonneuve, Plateau-Mont-Royal, and Rosemont neighbourhoods. Sherbrooke Street is a pretty boulevard that sweeps past the magnificent botanical gardens, one of Montreal's wonders, located just across from a disaster, the infamous Olympic Stadium, one of former mayor, the late Jean Drapeau's delusions of grandeur. Drapeau had commissioned his friend Roger Taillibert, the renowned French architect, to create the tower he had dreamed about. Each time I see this gigantic white elephant, I think how great it would be to let the Armed Forces practise on that mountain of concrete and reduce it to a pile that neighbourhood kids could use for tobogganing. But such considerations weren't about to darken my thoughts on this pleasant morning.

When I drove into the *Journal de Montréal* parking lot a little before 11 A.M., I didn't notice a young woman wearing earphones taking a coffee break there, smoking a cigarette. Since I was going to be leaving a few minutes later, I parked in the middle of the lot, in one of the spacious and well-marked spots instead of the area at the back set aside for *Journal* staff. Nor did I see a white car parked in the adjoining lot that belonged to a company that had just closed down. Nor did I notice the shifty individuals keeping close watch on the neighbouring streets, nor the man who, large blue umbrella in hand, was heading towards the middle of the parking lot.

As I was about to take my laptop out of the trunk, I felt as though someone had hit me in the back with a baseball, at the height of my right shoulder blade.

It was a terrible blow.

In a thousandth of a second, I heard shots. I remember the sound more than the pain from the impact of the bullets in my back. The shots were fired in rapid succession. I knew I had been hit by gunfire. Though I didn't count the shots, and never even thought about it, I realized I had been hit by several bullets.

The killer, because that's what he was, had fired on me seven times.

I was hit by six bullets.

The whole episode lasted barely two seconds.

The two most horrible seconds in my life.

Though I later found out that the weapon used for the crime was equipped with a silencer, I heard a loud, muffled noise. The gunshots seemed loud to me, but the young woman standing nearby neither heard nor saw anything.

Before the shots had even stopped, I turned to the right and saw, about three metres away, a rather young-looking individual wearing black pants, a black-and-white polo shirt, and a black cap. I saw a puff of grey smoke, about fifteen centimetres in diameter, at the height of his belt, to his left. I have absolutely no recollection of his face.

He didn't say a word but, keeping his eyes on me, headed east, towards the white car in the other parking lot. Why did he leave the scene while I was still standing? Did he, at the last moment, spot the young woman a few metres away? I often ask myself these questions, without being able to answer them.

I wondered whether the gunman was someone I knew. Already, I had in mind an idea who it could be, a despicable individual who became, following a previous career, a biker henchman. But the gunman's appearance did not match that of the man I had in mind, a rather rotund and paunchy fellow.

I understood that my situation was extremely grave. I knew it was up to me to call 911: at that time of day, in that part of the parking lot, there was very little traffic. It was unlikely that anyone would make the call for me.

At first, I grasped my pager instead of my cell phone. I then threw down the device and, because my back was sore, lay down on the ground to avoid making it worse. I then grabbed the cell phone hooked to my belt, pulled out the antenna, and punched in 911. For a moment, I thought the phone wasn't working because I was so close to the ground. But then a woman's voice asked the reason for my call.

"I've been hit by several bullets and I'm seriously wounded. I'm a journalist with the *Journal de Montréal*, the one who's handling the biker war," I explained. I also gave her the details about my condition, the location of my vehicle, and a very brief description of the killer. I added that he'd just run off towards the former Angus locomotive plant.

At first, the switchboard operator thought I was kidding. (I discovered this later when I talked to her.) How could a man claiming to have been shot so many times remain so calm? Though she momentarily thought this was a bad joke, she nevertheless initiated the procedure followed in such emergencies. She was typing the information on her computer as I was speaking, and the call was being relayed to the operator responsible for communicating with squad cars. Before I even ended the conversation, the Urgences-Santé ambulance and several police officers were on the way to the scene of this attempted murder.

The two or three minutes that followed were the longest in my life. I abruptly stopped talking with the operator as I realized that my condition was very serious and I wanted to conserve my energy. The operator kept talking, however, which is what she is supposed to do. Her instructions were to try to keep wounded callers conscious while help is on the way.

At the time, I had only one question in mind: was I paralyzed? I moved my fingers, my hands, my arms, then my neck, ankles, and legs. I felt pain on my right side, which I was resting on. I wanted to get up to see if there was much blood on the ground. All I saw was a reddish stain barely a few centimetres in diameter.

Did this exercise reassure me? I still don't really know. I

never thought about the possibility I'd die. Never saw the famous light at the end of the tunnel; still less did my life flash before my eyes. Perhaps my thirty-seven years as a journalist helped me. I've seen so many dead or wounded people that I instinctively knew what should be done.

Gunshot victims suffer enormously, but the pain is not as intense as you might think, given the trauma suffered by the body. I remember that one day, while tinkering about, I hit my thumb with a whopping hammer blow. The pain was excruciating. Though bullets do a lot of damage to the human body, its defence mechanism is triggered, blunting the pain. I would discover later that the pain was more intense after a few days in the hospital than in the moments following the attempt on my life. The brain secretes endorphins, a hormone that blocks pain, doctors say.

I had no option: I had to wait. Then, at last, I heard the comforting wail of sirens. Unfortunately, although I could see nothing from my prone position, I realized by the sound that the emergency vehicles had gone right past me. Probably they were heading for the second parking lot north of the building. Then I heard the sounds of braking, and of vehicle doors opening and closing. I heard a loud voice say, "There he is, in the middle of the parking lot." An Urgences-Santé technician approached. He told me not to worry. And then I felt the presence of several people around me.

One of the technicians, after cutting my beautiful new belt, began counting out loud. This wasn't a math exercise. He counted out loud and clear: "One, two, three, four, five, and six," for the number of holes he saw in my back and on the right side of my chest. One of the holes was, apparently, the exit wound from a bullet.

Dr. Suzanne Côté was with the paramedics and she immediately decided I should be taken to the McGill University Hospital

Centre, the former Montreal General Hospital, on Cedar Avenue. This is one of two hospitals in Montreal that has been designated to deal with trauma cases. McGill University Hospital Centre serves the southern part of the city, and the Sacré-Coeur Hospital the northern part. I heard someone ask whether bubbles were coming out of the bullet holes. They weren't. Apparently, bubbles would indicate that the lungs had been hit. The medical report shows that the wounds were sprayed with a saline liquid. This was the first time I'd observed such treatment, though I'd previously seen many gunshot wounds.

The emergency team acted very quickly. The doctor and her driver, technician Robert Boulay, had reached the crime scene so rapidly that they had to wait for the first police officers to arrive before heading into the parking lot. Côté later told me how horrified she was. She couldn't imagine how so many bullets had failed to hit an organ or artery. The wounds were extremely serious, but would not be fatal. Côté was also surprised by my calm. Ambulance driver Sylvain Caron was astonished that a man hit by six bullets could be making jokes. When he reported back to headquarters while I was still lying on the pavement and described me as a forty-five-year-old man, though I'm fifty-six, I turned around to say, "Thanks for taking a few years off my age." When Côté informed me that I was being taken to the hospital, I surprised her by making a similarly offhand remark: "I hope you take me to emergency rather than operate on me in the parking lot."

The whole response took place very quickly. According to Urgences-Santé reports, my call for help was received at 10:58 A.M., and the first vehicle, number 610, the one carrying the doctor, reached the scene at 11:02. Ambulance number 508 arrived near me at 11:04, and delivered me to the hospital at 11:20.

Throughout my career, I've seen hundreds of people on stretchers being placed aboard ambulances. Every time, a sympathetic pain runs through my body when the ambulance attendants shove the stretcher against the rear ledge of the vehicle to collapse the legs and wheels underneath. It seemed to me that the shock could be fatal to a vulnerable patient. I thought about this as the attendants lifted me onto the stretcher. As we neared the vehicle, I told them in jest about my fear of the fateful shock. Obviously, I lived through it. Nonetheless, whenever video footage of my transfer into the ambulance is replayed, I relive that fear.

I have a clear recollection of that ambulance trip, though I remember little about Côté, who was monitoring my condition, saying nothing. A technician held an oxygen mask over my mouth. I constantly tried to remove the device, which eased my breathing, but hampered my conversation. The vehicle was speeding along, siren blaring, lights flashing, a police squad car leading the way. I found the ride less arduous than I would have imagined.

Const. Trong Do was in the ambulance beside me writing down the phone numbers I was giving him to advise my family. Serge Labrosse, my immediate supervisor at the *Journal de Montréal*, and Yvon Tremblay, the head photographer, were in the front seat. Tremblay was there as much out of friendship as to do his job.

The information I gave was relayed to the newspaper's editor-in-chief, Paule Beaugrand-Champagne, and to her assistants, Andrée Le Blanc and Lyne Brisebois, who began seeking the personal addresses and phone numbers of my close relatives. My boss is the one who contacted my mother and my girlfriend. She also reached Pierre McCann, my long-time friend, who was immediately designated to break the news to Guylaine. Since she works in a medical environment, it was easy to ensure a doctor was by her side to support her when she got the news.

Poor Pierre! Thinking he'd dialled the cell phone of my son-in-law, Carl, an architect, he was surprised when Guylaine answered. He tried to convince her he was phoning about a problem with a building. Guylaine then exclaimed, "Whew! Good thing! I've always known that if something happened to my father, you'd be the one to break the bad news." Meanwhile, Pierre was discovering that footage of the crime scene was already being telecast. He was forced to tell the truth. A doctor and Guylaine's secretary reached my daughter's office with the news at the same time.

Ronald Saint-Denis is the radio monitor in the *Journal de Montréal* newsroom who follows what's happening on the police band and tracks the movements of Urgences-Santé ambulances and fire trucks. So he was the first person at the newspaper to get wind of the drama unfolding in the parking lot. It's not every day an ambulance is called to the vicinity of the *Journal de Montréal* as a result of an attempted murder. Saint-Denis immediately informed Yves Rochon, the news desk officer, and Chantal Murray, the secretary, then headed over to check for himself.

He went to see Alexandre Joseph, head of security, who glanced at the surveillance screens connected to the various cameras mounted inside and outside the building. At first, neither saw anything peculiar. We later learned that the cameras, whose quality was rather poor, couldn't monitor a strip of land about five metres wide right in the middle of the parking lot, precisely where I'd placed my car. Anyhow, even if the device had been able to cover that area, it still might have been impossible to see me since I was practically under the car.

At first it was thought a minor fracas or street fight had occurred near our offices, but still the editorial staff were on edge. Whenever a major event happens, you can feel the adrenaline flow in the newsroom. Everyone, from the messenger to the boss, wants to know what's happening. That's when a newsroom should be visited, to see how secretaries, clerks, photographers, and journalists get together, trying to discover everything so that their paper can be first and best with their news coverage. This is what was driving photographer André Viau, economics reporter Alain Bisson, and editor-in-chief Paule Beaugrand-Champagne when they rushed outside to see for themselves.

Bisson and Beaugrand-Champagne left through the main door, while Viau headed by a side door directly for the north parking lot. All three quickly realized there was nothing wrong there. Beaugrand-Champagne, who suffers from a hip problem, couldn't run. Bisson, a good athlete, headed for the other parking lot on the double. He only needed a thousandth of a second to grasp the magnitude of the event, and confirmed to the first police officers at the scene the identity of the man lying on the ground, shirt riddled with holes and stained with blood. "His name is Michel Auger. He writes articles on the Mafia and the biker war for the *Journal de Montréal*." The police officers' jaws dropped, according to my colleague.

Viau didn't waste any time either. He called out to Pierre Schneider, the arts and entertainment editor, who was trying to park his vehicle. Schneider didn't need a drawing to understand that Viau was serious. A journalist with more than thirty years' experience, he spent the better part of his life covering the crime beat. So both were also quick to approach me.

All were astounded that the drama we journalists and photographers seek elsewhere every day was happening in our back yard. The surprise was such that many journalists simply did not believe that the man stretched out in the parking lot was one of them. They thought that it was impossible for someone to want to kill a journalist here at home.

While medical specialists were tending to me, police officers were establishing a security perimeter. The news had already spread beyond my colleagues at the paper. Journalists from all over the city were converging on the Frontenac Street building. Martin Bouffard, a cameraman with the TVA network, was first on the scene. As a matter of course, he filmed everything. That's how, a few days later, I was able to see for myself how my colleagues and all *Journal de Montréal* employees were affected by what had happened.

Pierre Schneider, though he's seen it all, was completely stunned, as was Alain Bisson. Maude Goyer, our young colleague who would write the lead article on the murder attempt, was in tears before the cameras. Marc Pigeon, a new co-worker whose desk was next to mine and who was to replace me on several files, couldn't believe what he was seeing. Stéphane Alarie said in an interview that governments should wake up and reinforce the law. He said he was fed up with violence. My old pal Guy Roy, vacationing in the Eastern Townships, was reached by a television crew. Visibly shaken, he was trying to understand from afar what had taken place in Montreal.

Dany Doucet, the news editor, also appeared rather stunned, taking a few minutes to collect himself before returning to work. He's the one who would put the team into gear to "make a newspaper," as we say in the business. Nothing stops the publication of a daily. After assigning everyone their task, Doucet, I was later told, went out to walk in a park for two hours. Others went out for a beer.

The first police officers at a crime scene report back to their supervisors. When the crime is serious, many officers are dispatched. They are needed to protect the scene of the crime and to seek witnesses, both urgent police priorities in these situations.

Very often, the detectives who will handle the investigation are immediately assigned and are on their way too. Since the *Journal de Montréal* offices are in the northern part of the city, Chief Ronald Blanchette and Det.-Lieut. Normand Mastromatteo of the north end division initially took charge of the case. Because of the seriousness and complexity of the case, however, it was almost immediately handed over to detectives from the homicide squad. Officially, my attempted murder bears the incident number 38-000913-019 in the police archives.

As soon as he reached the scene, Det.-Lieut. Jean-François Martin of homicide took over. He in turn put Det.-Sgt. Guy Bessette in charge of the file. Bessette is rather portly, not very tall, and known for tenacity. A real pit-bull, according to his colleagues. His partner, Det.-Sgt. Michel Whissel, became the other principal investigator.

Lieutenant Martin surprised my bosses by requesting access to my voice mail to listen to the threatening message I'd mentioned less than an hour earlier. I'd laughed when I listened to that message the day before. Not that the woman affected by her spouse's death was wrong to complain, but I hadn't taken the call seriously. It was clearly a threatening message, but, given the character making it, I didn't think she'd hire killers to do me in as she promised on the phone. The woman was quickly charged and admitted her crime of uttering a threat. She posted bail and was able to regain her freedom immediately.

Another file I was working on intrigued the investigators. I'd just written an article denouncing the activities of a talented defrauder who'd got help from the Quebec government to create jobs in the Mauricie region. His name was Christian-Dominique Éthier. He had managed to get three organizations to pay for the funeral of his daughter who'd died of cancer. Among the generous donors were singer Céline Dion, who'd taken pity on the dying child, and a charitable foundation.

I was in a very good position to know about Éthier's past and machinations because he'd started legal proceedings against me for attacking his reputation. This lawsuit targeted both me and my bosses, the *Journal de Montréal* publishers.

In such cases, any self-respecting journalist carries out an exhaustive investigation for his defence. The research wasn't complicated, in this particular case, because Éthier had left a string of victims throughout the province. Many of the people I contacted hoped to be called as witnesses. "I've got lots to say about the fellow," they said. He had stolen from restaurants and building owners and bankrupted shopkeepers. He was also very well known in the clothing world, where he was establishing a new business when I published his story.

The judge ruled in favour of the paper in the libel case, but Éthier ended up in jail for another reason. He had tried to extort money from older men whom he accosted in the washrooms of shopping centres. Pretending to be a police officer, he told his victims he had proof they had committed indecent acts. Guilty people were ready to pay a fine on the spot. Others, innocent of any crime, paid anyway rather than risk public embarrassment. That's why he arrived at the trial to defend his reputation escorted by two or three guards. He was also handcuffed and wearing chains around his ankles, something not likely to impress a judge listening to complaints about an attack on his character.

After meeting with Éthier, investigators totally crossed him off the list of suspects.

An examination of the crime scene is crucial to detectives because it may provide a clue that will later be used to nail the killer. The image of Sherlock Holmes with his magnifying glass is not an exaggerated description of how specialists go about their business. They take photographs, shoot videos, look for fingerprints or any out-of-place item in a setting that is examined to the nearest centimetre. The process often keeps officers busy for hours. While lab specialists and criminal identification experts go about their work, other investigators look for leads.

At the scene of the attempted murder, Det.-Sgt. Michel Whissel found two cartridge cases from an automatic weapon, as well as a highly damaged projectile. Police officers first thought the gunman's weapon was a revolver. This type of weapon holds casings whereas an automatic one ejects them. As soon as they arrived, police seized the cassette from the surveillance cameras placed around the newspaper building. It was by viewing this video that they discovered the gunman got out of a white car parked in the adjoining lot. The man had walked behind other vehicles, trying to hide as much as possible, to approach me without my being able to see him.

Near the scene that morning, a bailiff was making his usual rounds through Montreal streets. He reached Gascon Street, near Sherbrooke Street, at about 11:15 A.M. His job is to locate vehicles whose owners have neglected to pay fines. He and his assistant install wheel clamps to immobilize vehicles belonging to culprits. The exhaust coming out of a particular car attracted his attention on this occasion. In fact, it was steam: the car's radiator had just burst. The vehicle was found seven hundred metres from the parking lot where the attempted murder had occurred. It was the getaway car used by the gunman and at least one accomplice. Pushed to the limit, the engine had overheated and the coolant lines had burst.

This second crime scene would provide the police with several clues. A .22-calibre pistol equipped with a silencer, an umbrella with a hole, a cap, and bullets were found either inside or near the car, which had been stolen two months previously from the city's east end.

News spreads very fast. The first reports broadcast in the minutes following the attempt informed the public I'd been wounded by two gunshots and that doctors thought I'd pull through. But few people seemed to believe the specialists. How, indeed, could someone survive two gunshots to the body?

At the crime scene, the police didn't know what to think of the gunman. Was he an amateur using a defective weapon? No one could explain how I could still be alive. An RCMP officer on a two-year assignment with the homicide squad was put in charge of contacting the hospital's surgeons and inquiring about their conclusions. Cpl. Pierre Thivierge remembers that the attending physician explained that all the bullets had lodged in a limited radius. According to the doctors, it was a miracle I'd survived. This specialist also told the investigator that he could practically describe the movement of my body during the shooting, based on the location of the bullets. I'd been extremely lucky while, thank God, the gunman had not.

A few days into the investigation, Det.-Lieut. Jean-François Martin was convinced the plot against me had been well planned and, especially, that it had not been staged by amateurs. He drew the same conclusion as the doctors. "The good Lord loves Michel Auger. His time hasn't come," he told a journalist. Martin also said he was optimistic about its outcome, and he confirmed that the motive for the attempt was directly linked to my profession and had nothing to do with my personal life.

I viewed most of the newscasts from September 13 in the days that followed, and carefully read the large dailies. A journalist with my experience knows all the tricks of the trade and can easily spot the weaknesses in media coverage. With the exception of the Hells Angels and their supporters, of course, all the experts blamed the attempt on organized crime. The police surmised, as did several reporters, that this attempt was the result of a biker plot.

There were two exceptions. One was reporter Claude Poirier, who claimed on Radio-Canada that I was probably responsible for what happened to me because of the tone and content of my articles. The other was Yves Lavigne, a Toronto author who's written three books on the Hells Angels and who's regularly solicited by the electronic media. Lavigne, who speaks in very provocative terms about the Hells Angels, often offers personal theories to explain events. That day, Lavigne was totally off the mark. He said that the Hells Angels were too sophisticated to carry out an attempt as poorly executed as the one against me. The police investigation, however, continued to target people directly linked to the biker gang . . .

It was 11:20 A.M. when ambulance number 508 reached the emergency ward at the McGill University Hospital Centre. Several people immediately surrounded me following my entry into the hospital. I was still unusually calm, doctors later told me, while they asked me numerous questions and technicians took X-rays or samples. They were examining my hands and feet, with a specialist for practically each of my fingers.

The operating room was ready in no time, and so was I. A doctor warned me that he might have to perform a colostomy and install a bag for evacuating stools, telling me I shouldn't be surprised when I awakened. One of the projectiles had perforated the colon and repairing the damage seemed difficult at the time.

The doctor didn't tell me about my real condition. He probably felt it was pointless to mention that two bullets had shattered vertebrae, without affecting the spinal cord. He also did not disclose the medical team's fears that there might be long-term complications caused by the bullet lodged against the fourth lumbar vertebra. One bullet had damaged the liver and spleen. Another had ricocheted off a rib, fracturing it, and exited through the thorax. Prior to being anaesthetized, I felt only a little heat in my lower back, as though something warm were spreading inside me.

After the first day, the media reported I'd been hit by five bullets. Doctors were talking about projectiles without specifying the number. A few days later, a police officer let the cat out of the bag in front of me, mentioning that six bullets had hit me. Detectives barely ever mention the calibre of the weapon used or the number of shots fired on a victim. Often, the only person with knowledge of such details is the assassin.

I really tried to establish the number of shots, but the task was impossible. I never managed to see all of my back. Moreover, the bullet fragments still embedded in my flesh, the bullets removed from my abdomen, and the one found shattered on a car rendered the arithmetic practically impossible. One of the bullets had been cut in two large pieces. Only six months later, when reading the detailed medical report, did I finally get a complete picture. I'd survived a volley of six bullets. Six bullets that had missed my vital organs. But with two bullets having struck the spine, it's a miracle I wasn't paralyzed. At times, only one or two millimetres spell the difference between normal life, paralysis, or death.

I thought I'd passed out in the emergency ward. In my vague recollection, I figured I'd spent only a few minutes there, so I must have passed out. But this wasn't the case. The medical report indicates I was taken to the operating room at 12:10 P.M.

The document mentions another destination directly beneath the line for the operating room: the morgue.

While the entire medical team was at my bedside, important security measures were put in place. Even Québecor's big boss, Pierre-Karl Péladeau, and his assistant, Pierre Francoeur, then executive vice-president of the Sun Media chain and publisher of the *Journal de Montréal*, were stopped at the hospital door. "No journalists here," is all the security guard said. My two bosses weren't laughing.

| 2 |

My Start in Journalism

Music is what led me to journalism. While in high school, I
belonged to a bugle band that took up my leisure time
and channelled my energy. As part of this band, known as the
Grenadiers-Kiwanis and consisting of sixty or so teenagers, I
learned to strive for my goals. Music was just an excuse for
members to get together. We'd spend our winters practising and
raising funds, and our springs and summers parading and, especially, participating in competitions. We were dazzled by the
exploits of similar groups in Ontario and the United States.
Through hard work, we managed to rank ourselves among the
best. Besides our desire to outdo ourselves individually and as a
group, we also had a common goal: proving to Shawinigan girls
that we were the best. Especially since a group from Preston,
Ontario, fascinated our belles.

It's this passion for the bugle band that led me, along with
my friend Denis Bellemare, to write a few columns in French on
the Quebec activities of these groups for a specialized English-
language paper published in the United States. This minor
experience led me to write a similar column for the weekly

La Voix de Shawinigan. Then a little later, I offered the column
to the daily, *Le Nouvelliste*, which had published a similar series
for several years signed François Guay, the heart and inspiration
of the Grenadiers group. Gradually, I understood that journalism was my calling. I even skipped class a few times to attend
public trials. One day, while an important coroner's inquest was
taking place in Shawinigan, the school principal decided to tell
parents that several students had played truant. He rightly suspected that they were at the courthouse. My father, Armand,
who worked nights, was pulled out of bed by my mother.

I was standing on the sidewalk when I saw my father suddenly appear. Without a word, he invited me to follow him to the
school and escorted me into the principal's office. I understood
from the principal's attitude that a second offence would not be
tolerated. Still, my curiosity about crime and criminals would
come in handy later on, and I began covering for *Le Nouvelliste*
the news-in-brief, the courthouse, and all the subjects felt to be
of public interest in a small town.

My first real teacher was Jacques Ébacher. He introduced
me to the basic questions every journalist should ask: Who?
What? When? How? And where? The first criminal case I
covered as a journalist concerned the disappearance of Denise
Therrien, a young girl from a good family who answered an ad
for a babysitter in Shawinigan-sud on August 8, 1961, then disappeared without a trace.

The remains of the sixteen-year-old student were found in
the spring of 1965, with directions from her murderer. Marcel
Bernier was the gravedigger at the Saint-Michel cemetery in
Shawinigan-sud. Using a false name, he'd placed the ad for a
babysitter as a trap to attract a young woman. He convinced the
Therrien girl to climb into his truck and tried to kiss her, which
prompted her to scream. He told police he panicked, hit the
teenager with a pipe, then buried her body.

A year later, he killed his mistress because she'd threatened to tell the police all she knew. Bernier had told her some secrets but, more significantly, she had found Denise Therrien's small red wallet. The gravedigger had also spoken carelessly to several other people.

Police had worked tirelessly for nearly three years to find the murderer. No one believed the girl had run away. Newspapers across Canada regularly reported on the affair, but no useful leads emerged. The provincial police's homicide squad, however, had had its eye on the gravedigger. Bernier finally confessed. Following his instructions, police officers dug up Denise Therrien's remains.

I wrote a few articles and took several photos of Bernier. He seemed never to regret his crimes and smiled most of the time I was with him. But that smile was wiped off his face on February 25, 1966, when Judge Paul Lesage sentenced him to the gallows. Though the death penalty was still on the books as the supreme punishment, Canada no longer applied it. Bernier died in May 1977 in a Western Canadian jail.

I remember seeing Bernier when I was a child – he was one of my neighbours. I had no way of suspecting he'd turn out to be a killer and that I'd have to write about his gruesome activities.

André Charest is in jail today for the 1986 murder of a Contrecoeur boy. He was a hockey instructor to eleven-year-old Steve Mandeville, whom he strangled with an electrical cord in his residence.

When I met him, Charest was only seven or eight years old. His parents owned a cottage near the one my grandfather had, in Saint-Gérard-des-Laurentides, a small town close to Shawinigan where we spent our summers. I later found out our former neighbour had become a petty criminal and a heavy drug and alcohol user. When assigned to cover the disappearance, then murder, of young Mandeville, I learned that a local hockey instructor by the name of André Charest was a suspect. Only on the night of his arrest by the Quebec Police Force (QPF) did I discover the murderer was my childhood friend. I phoned an investigator and got him to ask Charest questions about his childhood. The accused knew that his former neighbour, now a journalist, was covering his case.

During the trial, the accused's statement to QPF officer Jean Dagenais constituted overwhelming proof. Charest admitted to having consumed cocaine before the young boy's murder. Saying he'd been haunted by alcohol, sex, and drugs since adolescence, he admitted the crime, but swore he hadn't sexually assaulted the child, which the autopsy confirmed.

I was standing in front of him at a hearing before his trial when his lawyer asked that the proceedings be moved to some place other than Sorel, due to the population's hostility towards him in the judicial district where the crime had been committed. Charest looked at me without flinching, and seemed ill at ease. I testified at this hearing. I described the threatening behaviour of the crowd gathered outside the courthouse where Charest had been taken for his initial hearing. The request to move the trial was granted. Charest was sentenced to life in prison.

My initiation with the *Nouvelliste* lasted only a few months, and I then headed to Montreal, where I knocked at the door of Pierre Péladeau, publisher of several newspapers dedicated to celebrities, including the *Journal de Montréal*. He sent me to see his right-hand man, André Lecompte. As a greenhorn with only a few months' experience, I was excited to find myself among the great journalists. Lecompte, along with two colleagues, also had a career singing in bars and on TV. He was a member of the

Scribes, a group of humorists and commentators who specialized in giving their sarcastic views on life, politicians, and all
fashionable topics. Lecompte told me frankly that the *Journal de
Montréal*'s newsroom wasn't a place for me at the time. "You
don't learn a profession here, young man; you unlearn it. Go
and get some experience, come back later." And so I worked as
a journalist and jack-of-all-trades for a small publisher of maga-
zines for artists, then as a crime beat journalist with a daily
called the *Métro-Express*.

Métro-Express was a fine paper. It was founded by Jacques
Brillant, from the well-known Rimouski business family, during
one of the famous strikes that nearly killed *La Presse*. My experience there lasted nearly two years. The paper folded at the end
of 1966, the very day Muriel Rousseau and I told her parents we
were getting married. (Our marriage would end in divorce in
1991.) I had already begun to enjoy covering news-in-brief and
criminal investigations. Armed with a camera, I would drive
through Montreal streets, listening to the police band, heading
to the scene of interesting events. That's how I began to understand life in Montreal, to discover the city's recent past. That's
when I began hearing about crime bosses – the Cotronis,
Grecos, Obronts, and others – who were very active in the businesses and buildings of Saint-Catherine Street.

Every day my work led me to police station number 4 on
Ontario Street. It was the busiest police station in Quebec, a real
beehive, and rapidly became a good source of information and
subjects for photo reports. That's how my photos appeared in
various media. I became a journalist for CJMS radio, "the good-
guy team," as its slogan says. It was easy to combine activities as
a journalist covering the night beat with my role as a photographer. At the same time, I was contributing to the weekly
Dernière-Heure. I was gradually gaining experience and expanding my circle of contacts. I liked being constantly on the alert.

The adrenaline would flow whenever I'd rush out to seek the photo of the century, the news of the day.

I spent two years with CKVL radio before joining *La Presse* in May 1968. The daily was looking for a journalist with contacts and a genuine interest in crime news. Management wanted to hire somebody young who'd stick to that beat. Usually, young journalists start with the news-in-brief and, as soon as possible, move to another area. For a few years, while on the night shift, I also trained several colleagues who were starting with the paper, including writer Réjean Tremblay, who still hadn't dreamed up the characters of a popular Quebec television series, *Scoop*, that would make him rich and famous some fifteen years later.

While still a very young journalist, I got my hands on an important document, the first scoop of my career. This document would also bring about one of the worst days in my life.

A famous Montreal lawyer, Raymond Daoust, spent some time in Mexico with a bunch of local criminals taking part in one of the most important meetings of the international Mafia. This criminal lawyer had a great reputation in Quebec. He claimed to be the defender of widows and orphans, and bragged about having saved dozens of clients from the gallows. In those days, prosecutors were rated according to the number of murderers hanged, and defence lawyers according to the number of clients spared the noose. Lawyers weren't allowed to advertise at the time, but Daoust had managed to make a name for himself. He'd also amassed a large fortune in part, apparently, through shrewd business investments.

On March 3, 1970, *La Presse* published one of my feature articles on the front page, titled: "POLICE INTERRUPT COSA NOSTRA MEETING IN ACAPULCO." The subtitle: "THOSE QUESTIONED INCLUDE VINCENT COTRONI, (ETC.) AND MR. DAOUST."

The police had got wind of the Canadian mob's great migration to Mexico in February 1970, and had followed various Mafia emissaries from Montreal, Toronto, and Hamilton. Mob bigwigs had an appointment with the one and only Meyer Lansky, the American Mafia's great bagman. Participants all had one thing in mind: getting their hands on the casinos the Quebec government was about to legalize. Already, Montreal's mayor, Jean Drapeau, had started his own lottery to help subsidize the Olympics, the "voluntary tax."

Montreal Mafiosi were experts at illegal gambling. Notorious nightclub owner Vincent Cotroni was the local Mafia godfather. In fact, Cotroni managed Montreal's *decina*, a branch of New York's Bonanno family. They were associated with several Canadian and American bosses from the Jewish community. Cotroni, along with his family and friends, had made a fortune from illegal gambling in Montreal since the 1940s.

The widespread vice in Montreal had allowed a young lawyer, Jean Drapeau, and his colleague, Pacifique Plante, nicknamed Pax, to make names for themselves by fighting gamblers and crooks. With various religious and community groups, the two lawyers had put together a gigantic case against the criminals and their sundry associates who controlled gambling houses and brothels. Judge Francis Caron's inquiry uncovered a series of scandals implicating senior police officers and revealing suspicious links between politicians and criminals.

Following the investigation, Drapeau ran for mayor while Plante was appointed assistant director of the Montreal police in charge of the vice squad, which had emerged rather battered from the public investigation. But, after a first election, Drapeau was defeated in 1957 and Plante was fired. Though it was never disclosed publicly, Plante, the lawyer from a good Catholic family, had a few minor flaws. One of them was his fondness for women. Criminals set a trap for him using women of low virtue. Threatened with compromising disclosures, he chose exile in Mexico.

He and Drapeau, reelected in 1960, always remained on bad terms. It was only with the launch of the Commission of Inquiry into Organized Crime (CIOC) that Plante's honour was somewhat rehabilitated. He was one of the first experts to be heard. Meanwhile, the City of Montreal had increased his pitiful pension.

And so, the leading actors of Montreal's nightlife and underworld were in Mexico at this time, when the power of the political party that had dominated the province for years, the Union Nationale, was waning. The party was to lose power at the hands of the young Robert Bourassa and his Liberal team, elected at the end of April 1970. The criminals, who knew about Daoust's political connections, needed his help. Besides Meyer Lansky, those in Acapulco included major drug traffickers, murderers, and members of the Marseille mob. Montreal has always played a major role in dealings between Marseille heroin producers and American distributors. The French, who didn't get along with the Americans very well, decided to place their trust in the Montrealers. Hence the strategic importance Montreal has always had as a hub of international drug trafficking. The French connection was in fact the Montreal connection.

The police were keeping a watchful eye on this great gathering of mob bosses, as well as taking photographs. They followed the criminals to the villa of a former Montrealer. Leo Bercovitch, a millionaire who'd made a fortune in various legal and illegal businesses following the war, was now permanently settled in Mexico. This is where the gambling bigwigs met on several occasions.

Cotroni and his friends knew a fortune was to be made by exploiting gambling machines, card clubs, casinos, as well as in bookmaking and off-track betting on horses. But the Mafia's plans didn't work out, since gambling was legalized in Quebec and elsewhere in Canada. Finance ministers replaced Mafia godfathers in exploiting public vices. The most imaginative Mafioso would never have imagined amassing the billions of dollars now going into public coffers thanks to profits from lotteries and casinos. As a society, we can wonder whether it would've been better to give the Mafia free rein.

However, on that morning in early March 1970, such philosophical considerations were far from my mind. My article in *La Presse* was a land mine that would soon explode. In fact, it would blow up in my face. Raymond Daoust, the lawyer, called a press conference to deny his participation in the Acapulco meeting and to viciously attack the journalist who wrote the article and to threaten to launch a million-dollar lawsuit. Nonetheless, I was sure of my facts, which were supported by numerous verifications and a telex from Mexico reporting police activities and providing the list of characters questioned by Mexican police during the meeting.

That afternoon, I walked into the famous lawyer's office on Saint-Hubert Street, a twenty-five-year-old journalist not feeling very big in his shoes. Daoust, used to courtroom dramatics, was more than usually eloquent. He swore the whole story was false, that the journalist who wrote it had a wild imagination. Of course, he'd just returned from holidays in Mexico with his wife. Naturally, he'd met some of his clients on the street and at the beach since, like thousands of Canadians, they were vacationing in the sun. Never had he attended nor participated in any meeting of criminals. Loud and clear, he shouted that he was pure as the driven snow.

I knew he was lying through his teeth.

Daoust then pulled out a pile of documents proving him right. Among them were airplane tickets showing he'd already returned to Montreal when the police raid occurred the previous

Saturday. I was stunned. How could I have been so wrong? Was the telex I had bogus? Had I been set up? I didn't know what to think. Fortunately, an experienced colleague, Lucien Rivard, had been assigned with me to cover the lawyer's retort.

We printed the lawyer's denial on the front page. For a journalist, publication of an item contradicting what he wrote the previous day is a serious lesson in humility.

I wasn't out of the woods yet. How could we prove we were right? However often I went back to my sources, I always heard the same thing: "Daoust is a liar, he was there." Though I was right overall, the police report did contain some mistakes. In fact, there'd been several meetings among criminals in Acapulco, and not only one as the famous telex suggested. Moreover, several criminals and their friends had been closely watched but never questioned. This is what happened in the lawyer's case. Daoust had seen the weakness in our report and, like the crooked lawyer he was, had built his argument based on that weakness. After this experience, I never again could admire the theatrical courtroom gestures of certain lawyers.

The *La Presse* management assigned a specialist of the justice and police beat, Léopold Lizotte, to work with me. He looked a little like Columbo, the legendary TV detective, had a great sense of humour, and knew the world of lawyers and judges better than anyone in Canada. He was sent out to check the Mexican story, while Rivard and I tried to do some digging in Montreal. Our friend Lizotte got no further than we did. That's why, on March 28, *La Presse* followed up the lawyer's denial, published earlier, with a retraction on the front page in very visible boxed print. Its headline: "DAOUST NOT AT THE COSA NOSTRA MEETING."

It took me days, even weeks, to get over this affront. Such a blemish on the record is terrifically damaging. Colleagues single you out and doubt you for any old reason. How could I rebuild my lost credibility? Moreover, how could I prove the lawyer was a barefaced liar?

It took me several months to prove I was right. Shortly after the press conference, I was able to establish that Daoust had returned on a plane with a group of criminals and their wives. But this wasn't enough for an article. Then, some time later, I learned that a mysterious photograph had been seized during a raid at a Mafioso's home. This photo had been taken in a large Acapulco restaurant. Several criminals could be seen surrounding Vincent's brother, Frank Cotroni, including a mysterious unknown character whose head had been blotted out of the image.

When I obtained a copy of this famous photo, I managed to identify most of the characters in it. Cotroni's wife was sitting next to Raymond Daoust's wife. Both the unknown person and one of the criminals were wearing identical Mexican shirts. All those who knew of the photo thought the lawyer was the faceless person and that the criminal who had it at his place had altered it to avoid harming Daoust's story. A little later on, I obtained a series of photographs taken on the beach and in an Acapulco residence. They showed Daoust living it up with dozens of criminals.

It's in Ontario, however, that I finally found proof of the lawyer's deceit. An Ontario MPP (and former Toronto coroner), Dr. Morton Shulman, had got his hands on the complete report of the Acapulco affair and was disclosing its main points before the provincial legislature. Proof that I'd been right was finally made public. The MPP was going even further than I had: he identified Daoust as the Canadian Mafia family's adviser.

I travelled to Toronto in the midst of a snowstorm to get documents allowing me to write another article on the Acapulco affair. I was proud to be able to finish the job, even if I needed several months to do so.

3

The Cotronis

M ammola is a small town in Calabria, in the southern part of the Italian "boot." Built on a hillside, this European commune is a jewel of international heritage that includes several churches and a majestic cemetery on the other side of the hill. From a distance, you might think this was an extension of the town. When you stroll through the graveyard, you might be surprised to see a number of French inscriptions on the tombstones, such as *À mon grand-père untel* (To my grandfather so-and-so).

There's nothing surprising in this, however, since this southern village provided Canada with thousands of immigrants escaping wars and poverty, seeking their fortune and well-being in America. This generation of immigrants from the turn of the century quickly integrated into Quebec society. Within a few years, many French-speaking families bore Italian names. Grandfathers who had remained in Italy had grandchildren who spoke no Italian. These immigrants quickly took jobs that often had been abandoned by Quebecers. Accustomed to hard labour in their native country, these new Canadians rapidly became masters in several disciplines. The field of construction today comprises many craftsmen of Italian extraction. But the flow of immigrants to Canada also brought young people who chose crime over honest work. The Cotronis were among them.

In the early 1960s, nearly all young boys in Quebec knew that the Montreal Mafia boss was Vincent Cotroni, even though his name was neither written in the newspapers nor mentioned by authorities. When journalists talked about him, it was as a prominent businessman. And that was it.

Nicodemo Cotroni was a carpenter when he landed in Montreal in 1924. Little is known about him. The family, seven children in all, four boys and three girls, settled on Saint-Timothée Street as did several newcomers. The Cotroni sons quickly befriended local riff-raff. Life in the neighbourhood was tough. It was near the port and the red-light districts. The mob was already well organized.

With immigration also came the Black Hand, a sign used by criminals engaged in extortion. Under threat, minor craftsmen and shopkeepers had to pay "protection" money to avoid being beaten up or having their business destroyed. Most victims paid and hardly anyone filed a complaint or dared to denounce the criminals. These Italians, who knew very little about Canadian customs or the legal system, feared the criminals, aware of their activities in the mother country.

Vincent Cotroni prospered within this environment. Officially, he said he worked as an apprentice for his father, but he was arrested several times. He was most often acquitted and, if found guilty, always managed to get light sentences.

He partnered with wrestler Armand Courville and the two went on to important careers in Montreal wrestling. The effects of his wrestling career, however, marked his physical appearance for the rest of his days. It was as though his upper back

Back at work in the news room and feeling great, in January 2001, barely four months after the attempt on my life.

September 13, 2001: The first help has just reached me in the parking lot. I had been waiting for them impatiently for three minutes.

Urgences-Santé medical technicians start tending to me immediately.

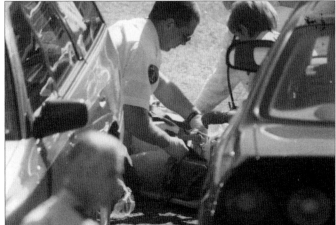

The ambulance attendants push the stretcher up to the back of the ambulance. The memory of the impact, when the stretcher strikes the rear bumper, still makes me wince.

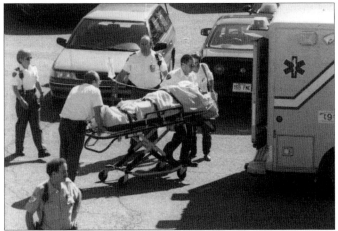

Claude Rivest, *Le Journal de Montréal*

The shock is visible in the faces of my colleagues in the *Journal de Montréal* newsroom shortly after the attempt on my life. From left to right: Pierre Schneider, Dany Doucet, Pierre Francoeur, Gilles Lamoureux, Serge Fortin and Paule Beaugrand-Champagne.

Claude Rivest, *Le Journal de Montréal*

Dozens of journalists from every medium rushed to the *Journal de Montréal* when news of the attack was broadcast.

The path the killer followed to reach my car.

The stolen car used by the gunman and at least one accomplice. It was found less than a kilometre from the crime scene.

The weapon used for the crime, a pistol equipped with a silencer, had been hidden inside an umbrella.

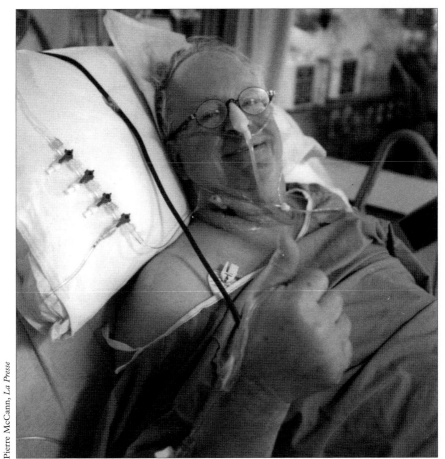

I asked Pierre McCann to take my picture two days after the attempt, so everyone would know I was recovering from my wounds.

André Viau, *Le Journal de Montréal*

This photo of Frank Cotroni's friends was taken in Acapulco. The criminal who kept it as a souvenir blotted out the face of lawyer Raymond Daoust, who swore he hadn't participated in the meeting.

Vincent Cotroni.

Vincent Cotroni with his brother Frank, his sister Palmina, and members of Paolo Violi's family, at a christening where Vincent was godfather.

The three Violi Brothers, Francesco, Paolo, and Rocco, all were later assassinated in Montreal.

Pierre McSween caused a sensation when he disclosed the hidden side of the war between his family and that of the Dubois brothers when he gave testimony to the CIOC.

Nicolo Rizzuto.

Vito Rizzuto.

A gambling house in the Saint-Henri neighbourhood is closed by police in the early 1970s.

The three CIOC commissioners became media celebrities in the late 1970s. From left to right: Judge Marc Cordeau, Judge Jean Dutil, and Judge Denys Dionne.

were fused, preventing him from turning his head without the trunk following.

Cotroni and Courville set out to make a fortune from illegal gambling, which they then invested in real estate and nightclubs. Cotroni acquired the Val-d'or on Saint-Laurent Boulevard, which became fashionable under the name Faisan doré. Though city nightclubs had previously offered mostly American entertainment, Cotroni and his associates featured French singers. The Faisan doré is where Charles Aznavour, Pierre Roche, Luis Mariano, Charles Trenet, and many others plied their trade. And where Jacques Normand showed his talents as an entertainer, along with several other Quebec celebrities of the day.

I knew Cotroni had mixed with both celebrities and politicians, so I used this as an excuse to solicit an interview with him. In my early days as a journalist, I didn't dare approach criminals for fear of running afoul of the police tailing them. Cotroni and his cronies were often under surveillance. At the time, I found him to be friendly but not talkative.

In 1964, *Maclean's* magazine and its Quebec counterpart published a lengthy series of articles on the Mafia and organized crime in Canada. The author, Alan Phillips, had placed Cotroni at the head of the Canadian mob. Cotroni filed a lawsuit against the magazine in defence of his reputation. The trial took place in 1972, and it's in the hallways of the courthouse that I first had a good conversation with him.

Cotroni talked at length about his career as an athlete and businessman. He explained the peccadilloes of his criminal past. But the man knew how to count and had amassed a fortune. He swore he could neither read nor write. He had just explained to the judge that he'd had some good luck at the Blue Bonnets horse track, and that his property was the product of savings and a few stock-market investments.

During the interview, this man, who was in his fifties and looked like anyone's grandfather, was courteous. Pacing the hallway, he kindly explained he had nothing to say in particular, that his life was very ordinary, that he was, in short, a very ordinary man and that police picked on him because he was Italian. I tried to get him to talk about Montreal in the 1940s and 1950s, but he said nothing controversial. I was disappointed because he could easily have talked about his experience as a youth and described Montreal nightlife back then. Following the war, Vincent Cotroni was at the heart of Montreal's hustle and bustle.

In the 1950s, the French mob was also present in Montreal. Cotroni was linked to Antoine D'Agostino, one of the French drug network bosses. Brothers Edmond and Marius Martin, Joseph Orsini, and François Spirito did a lot of business in Montreal, which caught the attention of police officers specializing in fighting international drug trafficking.

Vincent Cotroni was never arrested for heroin trafficking. Instead, he was involved in legitimate undertakings with the most important crime nabobs from all over. He held shares in Bonfire, a Décarie Boulevard establishment, whose owners turned out to be major mob bosses: Henri Manella and Max Shapiro had been associated with the underworld since the 1920s. Frank Petrulla was a Mafioso who disappeared mysteriously. Carmine Galente, who lived in Montreal for years, was one of the most powerful American Mafia godfathers.

Judge François Caron denounced the activities of all these individuals in his report, which exposed ties between criminals, police, and politicians in the 1950s. Cotroni had contacts among politicians. This was back when election workers were recruited among bar doormen and employees to get the vote out on polling day, at the municipal and provincial levels especially. According to his criminal record, Cotroni had only been caught for minor offences.

Though Cotroni got away from the police, his brother Giuseppe was caught red-handed trying to sell heroin to an American secret agent. Following ten-odd years in prison, Giuseppe returned to Montreal in the early 1970s, but never regained the position he'd held in the underworld before his arrest. Sickness also kept him away from family business.

It was in the mid-1950s that Vincent Cotroni began holding an important position in the local criminal structure. Many American gamblers and notorious criminals took refuge in Montreal as a result of an American Senate investigation led by Sen. Estes Kefauver. Godfather Joe Bonanno headed the active family in Montreal. He delegated his right-hand man there to take control of his business.

Carmine Galente rapidly made his mark on the underworld. He wasn't challenged since his two main assistants were Vincent Cotroni and Luigi Greco. Betting-house operators had to pay the organization for protection. His henchmen collected weekly payments on debts without having to break legs. Their reputation was established. The operation of the Montreal group run by major New York Mafiosi was only understood some fifteen years later.

Cotroni had no successor to take over his criminal activities. His daughter didn't get involved in the "business," while his only son, Nicodemo, born out of wedlock, had a rather pathetic, if not pitiful career in organized crime. Weighing nearly two hundred kilograms, the young Cotroni tried to use the family name to establish himself in the underworld. But his career never got off the ground, either in Florida, where he lived with his mother, or, later on, in Montreal.

The other Cotroni was called Santos, but the nickname Frank is the one that stuck to him. Though more talkative than his elder brother, from my point of view as a reporter, he had nothing useful to say. He was constantly surrounded by henchmen. In the

1960s, he was considered a disagreeable, reckless, and unpre-
dictable young man.

In the 1970s, Frank was nabbed for drug trafficking, tried in
Brooklyn, and then sent to prison for fifteen years. He had been
denounced for his involvement in a plot to import nine kilos of
cocaine with Giuseppe Pino Catania, a Mafioso who had moved
to Mexico and taken part in the famous Acapulco meeting.
During the investigation, police discovered that Frank was often
short of money and would desperately try to get rich through
transactions that frequently went wrong.

In August 1972, Frank Cotroni was arrested for extorting a
Saint-Hyacinthe restaurant owner. I was there when police collared him. I had my camera in hand when he left his home on
Place Chauvin, in Montreal's east end. His car had barely
moved a few metres when a police cruiser blocked his way. His
bodyguard and brother-in-law placed his hands on the car roof
– only one hand, in fact, since he had a finger driven up his nose.
Cotroni, seated at the wheel, was reading the arrest warrant a
police officer had just handed him. He saw me snap a picture of
him as he stepped out of his car, then started running towards
me. I took to my heels while a police officer grabbed his shoulder to stop him. My heart was pounding: I had just run the
fastest ten metres in my life. Later that afternoon, at the Saint-
Hyacinthe courthouse, Cotroni was constantly staring at me. I
knew this incident hadn't improved the Mafioso's opinion of
me. Extortion charges were dropped after a few days because
the plaintiff's memory seriously began to fail him. The story
he'd given police before the arrest of Cotroni and four of his
friends changed radically during his testimony at the preliminary investigation.

In the early 1980s, shortly after he came out of jail, Frank
Cotroni tried to reestablish his fortune through major imports.
He was captured two more times over drug deals and for the

murder of one of his colleagues, a police informer. His sons and daughter also tried to establish themselves in the underworld, but the Cotroni name wasn't enough to help them. One of the sons was murdered by minor drug-trafficking hoodlums.

Vincent Cotroni may have known he couldn't count on close relatives when he was getting ready to pass the torch in the early 1960s. So a young Calabrian living in Toronto, named Paolo Violi, became the godfather's favourite. Violi was short and stocky and used violence to get his way. He belonged to a family of eight children born to Domenico Violi, a Mafia guy, or so-called "man of honour" in his country. The family had immigrated to Canada and the United States in the 1950s. Four of the Violi sons settled in Montreal, and all of them were buried there. Giuseppe died in a car accident in April 1970, while Paolo, Francesco, and Rocco were later murdered in a war among families.

I was the only journalist present in late April 1970 when a hundred or so people, including most Canadian Mafiosos, gathered at the little Notre-Dame-de-la-Défense church to honour the memory of young Giuseppe. Armed with my camera and a telephoto lens, I stationed myself at the intersection of Jean-Talon and Christophe-Colomb streets, where the funeral procession had gotten under way. As was often done at the time, the family, the men especially, walked behind the hearse up to the church. I snapped a hundred or so photos. Each time a group turned at the intersection, I photographed it. Standing at the curb, I was very visible. No one said a thing to me. Examining my photos one by one the next day, however, I noticed that nearly half the criminals were looking at me with hatred.

I later tried to interview Paolo Violi, who almost laughed in my face. Knowing that police had bugged his Jean-Talon Street office, I had avoided going to see him there. His three grandsons were being used by the police and would help disclose the Mafia's greatest secrets. The information thereby gathered allowed members of the Commission of Inquiry into Organized Crime (CIOC) to infiltrate the Mafia's local organization in the 1970s. Montreal police were listening carefully when business was being discussed. This surveillance also allowed them to assess the strengths and weaknesses of the Violi brothers, as well as those of the Cotronis and other important mob bosses.

This eavesdropping was useful to me as well. Thanks to transcriptions of conversations I obtained, I was able to disclose Mafia secrets to my readers. Violi was puzzled; he wondered how an ordinary journalist could know so many things. "I don't get it," he told me. "How do you know so much about our business?"

But the Montreal police had been watching Violi's every move for several months. His office was a meeting place for criminals from across the country who would drop in to pay their respects to Montreal bosses. They would go to the back of the ice-cream counter and retire into his office to discuss financial business and family dealings especially. This surveillance provided police with a wealth of information. Violi was the Canadian family's number-two man at the time. Though Vincent Cotroni was the boss, Paolo Violi ran the daily affairs, making several enemies, as would later be seen.

One of those enemies was Nicolo Rizzuto, head of Montreal's Sicilian clan. In the criminal family's flow chart, the police had established that Cotroni ran four large groups. Frank Cotroni, Paolo Violi, Luigi Greco, and Nicola DiIorio were team leaders. Rizzuto, for his part, was only a subordinate who wanted to have his status upgraded. He didn't accept Violi's leadership.

At first, Rizzuto tried to further his own cause inside the group, where he had several allies. Violi, however, was unwilling to give up his power, which would be fatal to him in 1978. But at the beginning of the decade, a first major meeting of Montreal Mafiosos is what informed police that the local family was at loggerheads. Organized-crime specialists had tailed delegates to a summit conference in Gerlando Caruana's residence on Imperia Street. This house was located in the so-called Italian neighbourhood, in L'Épiphanie, in northeastern Montreal. Using a search warrant against the operation of a gambling house, police raided the place at 11:55 P.M., on December 14, 1971.

Twenty-seven people were on the premises, five of whom were playing cards. Four hundred and eighty-two dollars were seized on the table. The most important crime bosses of the last thirty years were present. All those the police identified as Mafia "men of honour" were there. Five of them would be murdered over the years, and many others would end up in jail or be accused of drug trafficking in Italy, Switzerland, the United States, and Canada. The police knew that major questions of the day were being discussed at this meeting, including the role of Nicolo Rizzuto, who'd gained strong supporters inside the international Mafia. His associates were establishing the most important drug-trafficking network the world had ever seen. Rizzuto had ties to the Caruana and Cuntrera families, who were in the news between 1980 and 2000 in Europe, South America, the United States, and Canada.

Leonardo Caruana, who attended the meeting, was deported from Canada because of his links to criminals. He was murdered in Palermo on the wedding day of one of his sons. Pietro Sciarra, another Sicilian boss posted in Montreal, was also murdered in that city. This individual, as would be discovered through CIOC hearings, had played a double game. He told one story to his Sicilian buddies, but police eavesdrops used by the CIOC showed he wasn't being frank. As he was leaving an Italian movie theatre belonging to the sister of the Cotronis, where he'd viewed the Italian version of *The Godfather*, he was

gunned down with a Lupara, a short-barrelled shotgun used by
Sicilian peasants and shepherds. It's the preferred weapon of
Mafiosos, and an integral part of their gear. Apparently, the
meeting in L'Épiphanie had not been enough to solve the organization's difficulties.

Throughout 1972, representatives of New York's Bonnanno
family and delegates from the Sicilian Mafia travelled to
Montreal to try to settle the issue of the refractory Rizzuto. All
those who sided with Violi on this issue were murdered, as were
he and his brothers. The head of the Agrigento family, Giuseppe
Settecasi, who'd travelled to Montreal to solve this problem, died
from bullet wounds. The remains of Carmelo Salemi, one of his
representatives, were found about ten years later in the trunk of
his BMW, which had been buried at the bottom of a quarry.

On November 29, 1973, I wrote an article for *La Presse* on
the internal workings of the Montreal crime family. I related
how the local group was in fact a *decina*, a branch of New York's
large Bonanno family, identifying all the leaders and describing
their responsibilities within the organization. What I didn't
know was that, in the days preceding publication of that article,
the same characters I was writing about had returned to
Montreal to again discuss the Rizzuto case. The information
and documents I had were a year old, but the problem had
remained precisely the same. A journalist can have the best
timing without knowing it.

I wrote another article with my friend Jean-Pierre
Charbonneau for *La Presse* on March 25, 1976. In it, we revealed
that a contract had been taken out on Violi, and gave an account
of a number of recent settlings of accounts against friends of
Violi or Rizzuto. We were clearly explaining what was at stake in
this war within the upper levels of the local Mafia. As well, we
mentioned that the old conflict between Violi and Rizzuto,
which everyone thought had been settled by New York and

Sicilian emissaries, had been rekindled by revelations made at CIOC hearings. Recordings of private conversations between Violi and his friends, heard by the commission, had disclosed compromising discussions.

When I accidentally bumped into Violi on Jean-Talon Street a few days later, the man known as the "Lord of Saint-Léonard," expressed skepticism about what we had written. "You write any old thing," he said confidently. He pretended to not believe the "novels" reporters invented. He also claimed he was absolutely unafraid of anything or, especially, anyone.

A little less than two years after this meeting, on January 22, 1978, Paolo Violi was murdered in his former store on Jean-Talon Street. He'd been invited there for a card game. Two individuals, lurking nearby, awaited the opportunity to discharge their Luparas into their prey. Violi died on the spot. In the minutes that followed, a call was made to Venezuela to inform Nicolo Rizzuto of the latest news from Montreal. "The pig's dead," the Montrealer said.

In February 1977, Francesco Violi was executed in his Rivière-des-Prairies home. And, on October 17, 1980, the last Violi living in Montreal, Rocco, was also murdered in the kitchen of his own home. The killer, armed with a rifle, had taken position in a next-door office building, where he waited several hours for his victim.

After following and writing about the criminal career of Domenico Violi, and that of his sons, I later began to cover the early dealings of a third generation of Violis, Paolo's children, who'd eventually be arrested for cocaine trafficking. Perhaps heredity would explain this penchant for crime. As for Vincent Cotroni, he died of cancer on September 18, 1984. A few weeks earlier, I'd visited with Palmina Puliafitto, sister of the Cotronis, to make another request to interview Vincent. She explained that he was unfortunately not able to communicate easily, and requested as a favour that I hold off writing about her brother's agony, which I agreed to. Then, a few hours following his death, I was invited to the Cotroni home to meet the next of kin. The family also opened its photo album. Even police had good things to say about Vincent Cotroni after his death. The respect with which he was widely regarded saved him from meeting the same fate as the Violi brothers and a few other Sicilian criminals who had had the misfortune of getting in Nicolo Rizzuto's way.

| 4 |

Two Major Investigations

Research done by journalists often leads nowhere, because the information initially obtained either proves false or unfounded. Sometimes an issue doesn't make it to print even when the facts are proven. This happened to me in 1971, when I obtained precise information about the existence of a vast criminal network inside the construction industry. Though small-time crooks have always worked in the construction industry, the importance of the information I discovered was of almost unimaginable proportion. An entire section of the construction industry had been infiltrated by a well-organized criminal group.

André Desjardins was vice-president of QFL-Construction, a division of the Quebec Federation of Labour. His extortion network reached into most of Quebec's major construction sites. Desjardins and his henchmen had influence over private and public contracts. This was the beginning of a huge journalistic investigation that prompted the Quebec government to create the Commission of Inquiry on the Exercise of Union Freedoms headed by Judge Robert Cliche.

But readers of *La Presse*, my employer at the time, had been denied this scoop. The news director back then, Yvon Dubois, had told me my articles were incomplete, that they disclosed details about the private lives of certain union officials, details that weren't necessarily of public interest. Even after I rewrote the articles, he still felt they didn't have enough substance to warrant publication. To finish the job, he assigned a colleague with much more experience to help me find a way to flesh out the document. This journalist was notoriously the laziest one in the newsroom. My great report was never used.

Later on, I understood my boss's apprehensions. He didn't want to launch a frontal attack on the QFL, whose affiliated unions had just caused two major strikes at *La Presse*. The articles for this series, which I've kept, were in fact incomplete, when judged in light of my present experience. They were dynamite nonetheless. In today's competitive world, articles of this type would likely be used by all major news outlets. But this was 1972, shortly after a strike that *La Presse* management thought would kill the paper.

I'd put together this important file using information gathered from police and criminal sources. André "Dédé" Desjardins was business manager of plumbers' local 144. He placed his friends on major construction sites, ran illegal lotteries, and managed a usurious moneylending network. He also ran a nightclub on Saint-Hubert Street and had personal and business ties to all the major Mafiosos of the day. Condemned for armed robbery, he afterwards obtained a pardon but never felt any remorse. His network was expanding by the day, spreading to other unions, including that of heavy-machinery operators, glaziers, etc. He wasn't the only crook to have infiltrated unions, but he'd managed to set up a network earning him hundreds of thousands of dollars.

In the course of my research, I had met Desjardins's adversaries on construction sites, the staff of CNTU-Construction, a division of the Canadian National Trade Unions. When I asked for help with my research, the two union-federation officials involved in the file greeted me with open arms. Florent Audet, an old trade unionist, and Michel Bourdon, a former CBC journalist turned union activist, already knew that some of their QFL opponents were crooks, and were delighted that this was becoming public knowledge. They gladly agreed to help and put me in touch with people from the industry who also had complaints about Dédé and his friends.

The file got even more substantial when I obtained several photographs of Dédé Desjardins vacationing in the sun with various criminals and his friend Louis Laberge, president of the QFL. One of the individuals photographed had kindly provided police intelligence services with the snapshots. Nicknamed Valentino, the man was constantly in Florida, from where he informed his police contacts about events in the Quebec crime world, then very active in the southern United States. This Valentino also became my informer. A salesman of police-band descramblers, this Anjou citizen included me on his list of correspondents.

When *La Presse* decided not to publish my articles on crime in the construction industry, CNTU officials decided to tell all at a press conference. The government was then compelled to create a commission of inquiry. The James Bay construction site had been vandalized, with part of the facilities being completely destroyed. A union representative was condemned for the misdeed and got a heavy sentence. This man decided to study law while in prison and, following his release, became a lawyer who practices to this day.

Desjardins, for his part, had spent seventeen years in the construction industry. "André Desjardins was an extremely strong man, recruiting his staff from the mob. He was strong to the point that, after infiltrating unions, he subjugated them to his ends, using threats, violence and blackmail against both workers and management. . . . In the face of such strength, too many contractors despaired of the law's inadequate protection, yielding to blackmail, with some politicians following suit. His exceptional qualities as a leader, strategist and organizer are wasted by an unbridled lust for power. This passion controls him to the point of destroying his moral sense. To him, there are no bad methods, only inefficient ones," said Judge Robert Cliche in his 1975 report.

Premier Robert Bourassa had appointed Judge Cliche to head this investigation. He was assisted by two commissioners, one from the labour movement, the other from the business world. The judge's two assistants, Guy Chevrette and Brian Mulroney, went on to very notable political careers. The commission's chief prosecutor was Lucien Bouchard, who went on to become premier of Quebec, after following his friend Mulroney to Ottawa.

In November 2000, Bouchard remembered the tough Dédé Desjardins very well. Bouchard said that the former union official had given him a run for his money during the 1974 public inquiry. "I questioned him for three days," recalled Bouchard during a conversation I had with him. At the time, Desjardins feared no one. He'd headed a group of construction workers who'd stormed the Quebec assembly right in the midst of a parliamentary committee. He was a master at controlling interviews with journalists, and loved to say he was devoted to his members. Although this was true, his methods were deplorable. It took years for the QFL to renounce Desjardins, whom its president, Louis Laberge, had defended to the end. He was ultimately banished from all union positions and resumed his criminal career full-time.

Though he'd once been a jeweller, he made a living mostly as a loan shark. "He liked money too much. Always wanted more. Couldn't get enough of it," one of Dédé's friends said. Desjardins moved to the Dominican Republic, where he was a hotelkeeper. The day before he died, he met with Hells Angel Maurice Boucher in Montreal. He was killed with eleven bullets, five of them to the head, while leaving a Saint-Léonard restaurant.

The weapon used by the killer was a .22-calibre Ruger-type pistol equipped with a homemade silencer. Exactly like the one a certain gunman used in the parking lot of the *Journal de Montréal* barely five months later, to do in a troublesome journalist. Gunsmith Michel Vézina was taken before a judge, accused of having made both weapons.

At about the same time the government created the Cliche Commission, it also created the Commission of Inquiry on Organized Crime (CIOC), whose activities would keep journalists covering the police and court beats very busy. As soon as preparatory work for this major investigation began, squabbling set in among police organizations, united under a single authority for the first time. Police from Montreal, the QPF, and the RCMP had great difficulty working together.

It was known in certain circles that a Liberal Party of Québec (LPQ) minister had had conversations with Mafia emissaries through a political organizer and innkeeper from Montreal. Justice Minister Jérome Choquette, who had created the commission, never made an explicit link between political scheming and the launch of the inquiry. Many, however, understood that the minister, just like his boss, Robert Bourassa, had wanted to neutralize the mob's efforts and send a serious warning to the party.

Moreover, Minister Choquette was receiving comprehensive reports showing that the Mafia and other large criminal organizations were becoming more pervasive in our society. Chief-Insp. Hervé Patenaude of the QPF was in charge of informing the minister about organized crime. He received information from other police services, as well as from two Montreal police officers, Asst.-Dir. André Guay and Det.-Sgt. Alphonse Gélineau. The latter was in charge of the vice squad for downtown, the squad dealing with "petty morality," as it was called in legal and police circles. Ever since the scheming of the 1940s and 1950s, police had set up several vice squads to try to counter corruption.

Gélineau, nicknamed Loulou, didn't easily take orders from his bosses; he was pretty much a loner who did as he pleased. During a search of a Sainte-Catherine Street bar, he'd got his hands on thousands of cashed cheques linking all the bigwigs of illegal gambling and the Mafia. He'd managed to convince his bosses, Guay as well as Patenaude of the QPF, about the importance of his find. This is how Project B was born, which led to the creation of the CIOC.

After a very rough start, the inquiry reorganized itself in 1975 under the direction of Judge Jean Dutil, who'd just completed his assignment as prosecutor for the Cliche Commission. He was assisted by Judges Denys Dionne and Marc Cordeau. Since its creation, the CIOC had done research in several areas, including betting networks, Mafia involvement in the cheese industry, political corruption, as well as the traditional organized-crime families. Commissioners wanted to know why the family of Mafioso Joe Bonanno was present in Quebec. Bonanno, one of the five most powerful leaders of the American Mafia, had already admitted to investing in a company belonging to Montrealer Giuseppe Saputo. The former's son Salvatore and some of his associates were often seen in Montreal at the Saputo company.

Interesting documents had been seized by Montreal police on May 18, 1972, during a raid at the Saputo cheese factory, in the Saint-Michel neighbourhood. Suspecting that health inspectors weren't doing their work properly, police with the organized-crime division had asked for help from a McGill University microbiologist to inspect Saputo pizza cheese. I was present at the raid, having followed police officers onto the premises. The matter caused a sensation.

Police officers jumped for joy when they found a suitcase containing personal documents belonging to managers of the company. They thought they'd found proof that Joe Bonanno still owned shares in the company, something that principal administrator Emmanuele "Lino" Saputo later denied. He testified under oath that the confiscated document was a note on profit sharing among members of the owner's immediate family. The inscription *Mr. J. B.* wasn't linked to Bonanno, he said, but referred instead to his brother-in-law, Joe Borsalino. No one ever found out why this brother-in-law owned more shares in the company than all other family members. The CIOC looked into this file behind closed doors, and never held public hearings afterwards.

The CIOC hearings were marred initially by quarrels and controversy. Public opinion was far from being impressed with the commission's work. However, under Judge Dutil and his chief prosecutor, Réjean Paul, the commission gradually managed to regain its credibility. The exposure of organized crime's role in the meat-packing business improved the commission's image. It turned out that the business was so corrupt that tainted meat was routinely finding its way onto Quebecers' tables. For the first time, television cameras were admitted into the courtroom. Cable companies were the first to benefit from this. News company managers were pulling at their hair over the high ratings enjoyed by community television that, until then, had

broadcast amateur entertainment and given voice to organizations more parochial than national.

Gradually, all of Quebec began to pay close attention to the
horror stories judges disclosed daily. When criminal bigwigs
were called as witnesses, the public was confident they wouldn't
get off easily. Those who refused to answer ended up in jail for
up to one year, the maximum sentence for failing to cooperate
with the court. Some criminals talked more than others. The
first CIOC informer was Théodore Aboud. The United States
had had Joe Valachi – first of the great informers and best
known of the penitents who'd disclosed all the Mafia's secrets –
and we had Aboud. He had dabbled in everything, though he
was primarily a specialist in fraud and major stock-market
schemes. I had obtained an exclusive on Aboud's collaboration
with the CIOC as well as a photo of him. Unfortunately for me,
this article was published on the paper's back page. The explanation was simple: the new boss who took office that day had
absolutely no idea about the importance of this news. He was
from the business world and had probably never read a single
article on crime. This gaffe certainly didn't hurt him, since he
subsequently became vice-president with a very large multi-
national corporation.

I made up for this disappointment later on by being the first
to get an in-depth interview with informer Pierre McSween
when he let the cat out of the bag before commissioners.

McSween caused a sensation when he appeared before the
CIOC. This white-haired henchman had been mixed up in the
war with the Dubois brothers, who were from Saint-Henri,
against the McSween family and their friends. The Dubois clan
ran the show in Saint-Henri and downtown. Since the early
1970s, this war had produced corpses nearly every week. The

CIOC had made the Dubois file one of its priorities, right after studying the Cotroni-Violi clan.

McSween wasn't a great thinker, but he had a good memory. His story was one of fights, gunshots, and blood. It was the story of betrayals, of plots on a very small scale, and of a violence that had escalated to the point that its protagonists didn't know how to stop it. McSween confided to me that he'd decided to avenge his brother who was murdered by the Dubois clan. Rather than pursue the vendetta on his own, he decided to reveal everything to get even with the Dubois. The inquiry would show that the nine Dubois brothers trafficked in drugs, extorted thousands of dollars, and had bar owners in their clutches. Their businesses were doing well, and everything was running smoothly until the CIOC hearings commenced. Then one day, Donald Lavoie, one of the family's killers, was cornered by his friends. During a meeting in a downtown hotel, Lavoie became convinced that his best friend, Alain Charron, and the Dubois brothers were going to shoot him. He escaped by jumping into a laundry chute.

He confessed as well. He told of twenty-seven murders, twenty-seven settlings of accounts, most of them linked to the illicit businesses run by the Dubois brothers. Many of these crimes were unwarranted. An innocent man was killed by mistake in Pointe-Saint-Charles, because he drove the same type of car as the man the assassins were mandated to eliminate.

The Dubois brothers hated the police, who returned the feeling. One night in November 1975, journalists were called to a strange press conference in the office of lawyers Rolland Blais and Sydney Leithman, who regularly defended the Dubois brothers in court. The Dubois brothers appeared naked before photographers. They had been given a good hiding in the police station and wanted to make it known publicly. Though they filed a complaint with the Quebec Police Commission, no reprimand was issued against anyone following the agency's investigation.

The Dubois brothers weren't too fond of journalists, though they had at least two in their pockets, including Claude Jodoin, a crime reporter with the *Journal de Montréal*. He was later fired when his bosses discovered his double-dealing. At the funeral of the Dubois' father, their sister got angry and, with two other family members, moved towards journalists and photographers. I then called out to Claude Dubois, the most visible of the brothers, who immediately calmed his relatives down. He asked to meet me later in the day to explain their anger.

Dubois took me to certain bars where, according to the CIOC, criminal incidents had taken place. Obviously, none of the individuals we met that day had anything to say against the Dubois brothers, especially in presence of the clan leader. Later on, Dubois was condemned for a double murder that took place in a Montreal North café, following revelations made by Donald Lavoie during his testimony before the court. He served his sentence and now lives in the Laurentians. The name of this family would have been all but forgotten years ago had the youngest brother, Adrien, not become one of Montreal's leading organized-crime figures. He also became a prosperous businessman, owning buildings and nightclubs in the Laurentians.

Ironically, the turpitude displayed by the Dubois brothers in corrupting the journalist Jodoin backfired on them. In fact, when Det.-Capt. Julien Giguère and his anti-gang squad took on the Dubois brothers after a string of murders, Jodoin sang like a canary. Following his career as a journalist, he became Claude Dubois's principal legal adviser. He even opened an office, hired a lawyer, and personally advised the criminals on legal matters. He died shortly thereafter, of natural causes.

| 5 |

Famous Criminals

Whenever I have spoken with friends or members of the West End Gang, they have always said the same thing: the gang doesn't exist; it's the creation of journalists and the police. They're almost right, in fact, because the gang has no formal structure and no chain of command. It can't be compared to the Mafia or biker gangs in any way. But the organization is well and truly active. It's an ephemeral association grouping certain characters for specific jobs or heists that are carried out and quickly forgotten. People come together for a period of time or to commit a crime and then move on. Most of those now known to belong to this group are involved in either huge robberies or major cocaine or hashish trafficking.

I've always been fascinated by this gang of hooligans who robbed only the rich. They had a great talent for detecting surveillance. Police were often a hair's breadth from making arrests, but repeatedly they managed to get through police traps. The Matticks brothers, the Johnston brothers, the McAllisters, as well as Paul April, Kenneth Fisher, and especially Allan Ross and Peter Frank Ryan all left their mark on Canada's criminal history. Some of them knew how to break into safes or vaults, while others used weapons to head straight for cash registers. Many of them were afterwards arrested for major drug imports, while their luckier associates enjoyed considerable sources of undeclared revenue undisturbed.

Montreal safecrackers have always been recognized as experts in the field. In the 1940s and 1950s, Lucien Rivard, Giuseppe Pep Cotroni, and their associates were masters at getting into the basements of financial institutions. Often, during long weekends, the burglars would dig tunnels and dynamite walls to get into vaults and make off with lots of cash, often the black money hidden from the tax man. Anglophone members of the West End Gang were experts at neutralizing alarm systems. The group's electronics specialists needed very little time to disarm even the most sophisticated systems. The number of major heists increased. Because the likely culprits were well known, however, the police also had considerable success.

Members of the gang were caught in Vancouver on January 9, 1977, after emptying the vault of a private company, the Vancouver Safety Deposit Vault. So confident were company managers about the strength of their vault's walls that they didn't even take the precaution of installing an alarm. In any event, no system could have kept out Ronald McCann, Paul Bryntwick, Talbot Murphy, Robert Steeve Johnston, or Kenneth Fisher. They were captured only because they were too sure of themselves. Even before the crime was discovered, a baggage handler at the Vancouver Airport alerted police about bags he felt to be suspiciously heavy. Large hockey-equipment bags were stuffed with bank notes, jewellery, and valuable certificates. The police nabbed the entire team. For once, police really were following a good lead.

On June 19, 1998, I learned that the Montreal Urban Community police's anti-gang squad was onto a very large heist.

Thanks to a good contact, I found police officers in the middle of a meeting in a Saint-Laurent cemetery. Though the names of suspects hadn't been mentioned, I knew members of the famous gang were involved. I mentioned two names when I spoke to Det.-Lieut. Robert Lamarre: Murphy and Fisher. I hit a bull's eye. However, I had serious doubts arrests would go as smoothly as police officers wanted them to.

The operation was scheduled for 5 P.M., and the duo showed up right on time at the home of a rich Mount Royal businessman who was thought to be on vacation. The two men expected this operation would provide enough money for a golden retirement. The police hadn't done any surveillance, awaiting the criminals, instead, in hiding places around the house.

The two malefactors parked their truck in the driveway as though they were a lawn-maintenance crew. After looking around a few times, they disappeared into the bushes. Detectives had decided to let the two thieves enter and then leave the house before intervening. Things began to happen in a great rush, however, when the owner of the house unexpectedly returned. The detectives made the arrests. Fisher, a construction hat on his head, and Murphy, with some document in hand, both said there had been a mistake, that they were honest people. However, they quickly understood they were done for. I tried to get their comments, but it isn't really the time for a journalist to ask questions. As so often happens, the two men and an accomplice got off with "exemplary" sentences, i.e., a few weekends in prison.

Allan Ross wasn't so lucky. He was convicted in Florida of being involved in major drug trafficking and murders, which ensured he'd spend the rest of his days in the safest of American prisons. He ended up in the worst of Uncle Sam's prisons with the likes of former Panamanian president Manuel Noriega and other significant Colombian drug traffickers caught by American justice. At least Ross survived his time with the gang, which wasn't the case for his predecessor at the head of the organization, Peter Frank Ryan, known as Doony. He was gunned down by one of his assistants, Paul April, but his loyal associate, Ross, had the traitor eliminated.

The crime was executed by a member of the Hells Angels motorcycle gang, who sent the traitor a VCR filled with explosives, with instructions to watch a video relating the biker gang's tumultuous history around the world. April was hiding with three of his friends in a Maisonneuve Boulevard apartment. The time was November 1984. A few moments after the VCR had been opened, a powerful bomb was triggered from a distance, instantly killing April and the three henchmen hiding with him.

I went over to the site shortly after the explosion. It was a miracle that no one else died. The walls of ten or so apartments had been completely destroyed and debris had flown in several directions. Other occupants of the floor had escaped with minor scratches and injuries. Ironically, the hideout where the four murderers had stayed was right in front of former police station number 10 at the corner of Saint-Mathieu Street.

Journalists assigned to cover police business get to rub shoulders with criminals, or at the very least meet them as a matter of course. Encounters with bigwigs are sometimes a letdown, but other criminals who aren't as well known can turn out to be fascinating characters. Fraud artists are surely in a category of their own. Names like Laurier Boutin or Gilles Denis once made headlines, but have probably been forgotten.

Gilles Denis was a kind of Robin Hood who stole from the rich and gave to the poor. Like the mythical Robin Hood, he also always had a good time. He was especially active in the 1970s both in Canada and in a number of Latin American countries. Though he was sometimes called Father Denis, "Monsignor" is the title he used most of the time. This ordinary Quebecer with little formal education wore a cassock, took confessions, and did good deeds. He was, however, very daring and could convince anyone about anything.

After defrauding close relatives, he fled to Peru in 1972. He was arrested there driving a stolen car and was imprisoned. In a short while, he was saying mass, confessing guards and prisoners, and preaching the good word. Afterwards, he took great pains to get rich Quebecers to fund charitable works. Several doctors were fooled by good Father Denis into making considerable donations, some of which were actually used to set up various services. At one time, however, he gave up good causes to traffic cocaine between Quebec and Colombia. He convinced some of his altar boys to make small deliveries, but his game was foiled by a police officer with a good nose, a certain Guy Ouellette, who later became Sergeant Ouellette, the QPF's expert on biker gangs.

Laurier Boutin, for his part, was a genuine mythomaniac. He loved taking people for a ride. At different times he pretended to be a terrorist, a Mafioso, a deputy minister of justice, and a heart surgeon. Absolutely nothing made him flinch. If he were still alive, he'd be at least seventy-two years old. This man had gulled dozens, if not hundreds of people, and spent several years in American and Canadian penitentiaries for exercising his talent.

In September 1972, Winnipeg newspapers featured a story about the son of Joe Colombo, the notorious New York Mafioso. The story was accompanied by a photograph of the criminal standing in front of a mansion he'd just purchased from an heir to the famous Eaton family. Joe Colombo, Jr., was also announcing his wedding to a Winnipeg girl. He claimed that he had left New York because his father was too famous. He also announced, to everyone's surprise, that he had invested heavily in the World Hockey Association, which had just been created to compete with the NHL.

The news made headlines in Montreal too, especially in the *Montreal Star*, which published the story and a large photo on the front page. The head of the Montreal police's fraud squad, Det.-Capt. Léon Saint-Pierre, is the one who exposed the story as a fraud. He recognized one of his former clients, Denis-Laurier Boutin, an imposter who had given him headaches for years. The Colombo family also denied any knowledge of or connection with this character in Winnipeg. Boutin was promptly put on a plane to Montreal, since arrest warrants had been issued against him.

He was affable and relaxed when he was arrested at Dorval airport and taken to the fraud squad office, on the second floor of police headquarters at 750 Bonsecours Street in Old Montreal. With help from Captain Saint-Pierre, I was able to meet Boutin in a small interrogation room there.

Boutin was glad to talk. He laughed at the joke and the consequences of his Winnipeg scheme. He seemed to be quite pleased with himself. Then, drawing closer to me, he told me that people hadn't seen anything yet. He said that he had hidden important documents in Winnipeg. He claimed that their contents were truly explosive. Taking me into his confidence, he revealed that he had hidden them in the suspended ceiling of a closet in his Winnipeg room. "All you have to do is go and get them," he said.

I still remember Captain Saint-Pierre's broad smile when I emerged from the interrogation room. "And so?" he inquired.

He fell over laughing when I told him about Boutin's claim. I had been ready to leave for Winnipeg myself, but Saint-Pierre said, "I'll call my colleagues in Winnipeg and ask them to search the room."

We rapidly got the answer Saint-Pierre expected: there was

nothing there. I later asked Boutin why he'd tried to fool me. "For the fun of it," he answered.

I wasn't the first to be taken in by this storyteller. He once convinced a senior provincial police officer that he was the deputy minister of justice. He asked that a squad car pick him up at the ministry's offices in Quebec City and drive him to Montreal with the utmost urgency. The imposter then simply headed to the waiting room at the ministry on Grande-Allée Street, where he told the receptionist his name was Boutin and that he was waiting for a police officer. When the officer showed up and asked to speak to Deputy Minister Boutin, the good receptionist introduced him to the citizen who was seated there, reading a document. This is how Boutin showed up at a bank and then a car dealership in Sorel to commit fraud while under police escort.

He later used the name of Chief Justice Édouard Archambault of the Court of the Sessions of the Peace to cash a few cheques. On another occasion, he pretended to be a guerilla and friend of Fidel Castro and Che Guevara. Held prisoner in an American jail for illegal entry into the United States, he was called before a Senate committee investigating an explosion that killed a dozen people at La Guardia Airport. He refused to testify, pleading the American constitution's Fifth Amendment. In the plane returning him to Montreal on November 18, 1976, the crew discovered a note claiming a bomb had been placed on board and demanding the aircraft be immediately diverted to Cuba. Only much later was Boutin accused of this attempted hijacking. His fingerprints were found on the note. He was sentenced to seven years in jail. But before disappearing, he convinced a few journalists that he was a victim of his political opinions and Quebec's first genuine political prisoner. Since then, no one has heard a thing about him.

Lucien Rivard may have been the best-known and most-talked-about Canadian criminal of his time. He was one of Canada's biggest heroin traffickers in the 1950s and 1960s and the man behind a major political scandal that nearly brought down the Pearson government. I scored a journalistic coup in the case of Rivard when that scandal was dominating the national news. Rivard's story became famous around the world. At the time, people said that he'd escaped from the Bordeaux prison by claiming he wanted to water the outside skating rink, though the temperature was very warm at 4°C. Rivard has never wanted to reveal his secret, but the story about watering the rink was only for the peanut gallery. In fact, his escape had been facilitated by someone inside the prison. Following his jailbreak, he forced a motorist to give him his car, then vanished. Rivard had been held while awaiting extradition to the United States, where one of his carriers, having been caught with some $60 million worth of drugs, had decided to tell the authorities everything. Rivard's freedom lasted four months before he was caught.

A political scandal broke out when the aide to a minister of the Canadian government offered $20,000 to the lawyer hired by the American government to handle the trafficker's extradition. The political aide was sentenced to two years in prison for attempting to obstruct justice. The political career of several members of Lester Pearson's Liberal government was sullied by this scandal.

Rivard was imprisoned at the Lewisburg jail, in Pennsylvania, an institution holding 1,300 prisoners, where he was a model inmate. He worked in the kitchen. He knew a thing or two about restaurants, having for years operated La Plage idéale in Auteuil, an establishment frequented by several generations of young people.

When he was about to be expelled from the United States, many journalists, including me, were already in New York to attend Frank Cotroni's trial. Cotroni also was accused of importing drugs. The journalists I was with played a cat-and-mouse game there all week. Everyone knew that Rivard was to be deported the following Friday, but no one had any idea that everyone else was in on the secret. I was the only one who thought about the ruse of flying first class. Consequently, I had the pleasure of travelling from NewYork to Montreal practically alone with Rivard while about thirty of my colleagues – having purchased economy-class tickets – looked on in frustration from the back of the plane.

Of course, I chatted with the drug trafficker on the plane, and, as we were about to disembark, I offered to drive him wherever he wanted. To make my offer more persuasive, I picked up his suitcase and told him to follow me. Some journalists thought I'd signed an exclusive contract with Rivard to write his memoirs, but I was simply opportunistic. This is how Rivard and I took a taxi for the north of the city, where Marie, his wife, had patiently awaited him for several years. Rivard told me he was only passing through Montreal and that he intended to settle somewhere in the sun. As for his memoirs, Rivard never considered writing them. He preferred to keep all his secrets to himself. Had he chosen to relate his life, the story would've been thrilling, since he was a pillar of the Montreal mob. A safe-cracker in the good old days when banks were robbed with acetylene torches, he knew all the political schemes in the small towns on Île-Jésus, as well as the secrets of many politicians. He would've had lots to say. He finally settled into a condominium on Patton Island in the Chomedy neighbourhood of Laval. He travelled on occasion. When I last heard, he'd aged a great deal and suffered from an illness similar to Alzheimer's.

I again wrote about the Rivard scandal in 1995 when I discovered that Bloc Québécois Leader Lucien Bouchard's Ottawa chauffeur was Gaston Clermont, a former Laval hotelkeeper and close friend of Rivard in the good old days. Clermont, Rivard, and their wives vacationed together. The police kept watch over Rivard and his friends. Clermont was then a prosperous hotelkeeper, the owner of a paving company, and, especially, an experienced political organizer. Rivard operated through him to obtain favours from certain MPs or ministers, such as a change of prisons or early parole for another heroin trafficker.

I was convinced that mere disclosure of the presence in Bouchard's close circle of a man who'd been mixed up in one of the greatest political scandals in Canadian history would make waves. Surely, I reasoned, exposure of this connection was of public interest since the man was paid with public funds. But my article caused scarcely a ripple. Bouchard didn't have time to meet me to discuss the Clermont affair. The Bloc Québécois' chief organizer, Robert Dufour, maintained that Clermont's earlier troubles were due to his being a nightclub owner and to some of his customers being known criminals. As for Clermont, he said he would quit his job as chauffeur and bodyguard if his presence were deemed harmful to Bouchard. Disclosure of this information had absolutely no repercussions, and Clermont continued to work for Quebec's most popular politician for many years.

Alvin "Creepy" Karpis was born in Montreal in 1908, but it's in the United States that he had a career as a famous gangster in the 1920s and 1930s. He's the one who allowed J. Edgar Hoover, the renowned FBI boss, to make his first arrest in May 1936. One month earlier, when he appeared before a U.S. Senate committee, Hoover had been insulted when a politician rebuked him for never personally making an arrest. Karpis later said that Hoover showed up when all risks had passed. "He was there for the photographs," he said.

In September 1969, when I interviewed Karpis, I had to get background information on the character, since I was too young to have heard about the capers of the gang he headed with Ma Barker. Karpis had just been expelled from the United States after having spent thirty-three years in prison, twenty-four of them in Alcatraz, the large West Coast penitentiary. Given his age, only one condition had been placed on his release: that he leave American soil.

Karpis was a hero to the criminal world between the two world wars. He was born in Montreal to Lithuanian parents and was called Albin Karpowitz. It's in Topeka, Texas, however, that he took his first steps in life and in crime, being first arrested at the age of ten. From reform schools to prisons, he wove a strong network of friends for himself among thieves. He notably mixed briefly with the famous robber couple known as Bonnie and Clyde. According to Karpis, Clyde Barrow was a vulgar assassin who loved to kill policemen, while his companion, Bonnie Parker, was an idiot. He didn't stay with them very long.

Karpis linked up with Freddie Barker when they both were in prison. The two criminals then distinguished themselves throughout the country as leaders of the Karpis-Barker gang. Freddie had four brothers, and his mother, Ma Barker, had become the worst criminal in the States, according to the FBI's big boss. The gang, including up to twenty or so members, robbed banks and kidnapped rich citizens to get large ransoms.

In his memoirs, published after his prison release, Karpis revealed that police had greatly exaggerated Ma Barker's role. She wasn't the leader of the terrible gang Hoover made her out to be. The FBI's director had written that Ma was "the most ter-rible, vicious, dangerous and intelligent criminal of the last decade." Karpis said that the woman had never been arrested and it wasn't an insult to her memory to say she had none of the criminal intelligence needed to oversee the gang of hoodlums of which he was a leader.

In the papers, Ma was nicknamed "Bloody Mama." On January 16, 1934, Ma and her son Freddie were surrounded in a cottage near Lake Weir, in the vicinity of Ocala, in Florida's heartland. Federal agents tossed tear-gas grenades, then barraged the place with heavy-calibre fire. Few gunshots came from the house. After a few minutes, Ma Barker and Freddie were found dead. He'd been hit by fourteen bullets. Karpis left Florida on the double.

Karpis ran into FBI agents in New Orleans in May 1936. He was coming out of a house unarmed, and was about to climb into a car when the police nabbed him. The officers hadn't even taken the precaution of bringing handcuffs, which made some people say it wasn't expected that the prisoner would be brought back alive. Karpis was bound with an officer's tie and driven to prison by J. Edgar Hoover himself.

When he returned to Montreal, a city that was completely foreign to him, Karpis was taken care of by the Salvation Army. When I met him the day following his return to Montreal, he looked like a kindly grandfather. He spoke little, but was pleased to relate his memories of Hoover, whom he thought poorly of, saying the FBI boss was always looking for publicity. He said he now only wanted to take advantage of life. He lived a short while in Canada before moving to Spain, where he died in 1979 at the age of seventy-two.

The Special Corrections Unit (SCU) was the prison for the real hardened criminals. It housed sixty or so prisoners and as many guards inside the huge Saint-Vincent de Paul prison in

Laval. Built in 1968 at a cost of slightly more than $2 million, it was a maximum security penitentiary holding escape artists and the most serious cases that the prison system couldn't handle elsewhere.

Crime celebrities met in this prison. The list is long, but the biggest names no doubt are those of Jacques Mesrine and Richard Blass, two characters with completely different pasts who shared the need to cause a sensation. Neither had any respect for the lives of others. Both wanted to help their imprisoned colleagues and both staged spectacular escapes. They became media celebrities and kept journalists busy for a long time.

Jacques Mesrine was born in 1936. He distinguished himself as a paratrooper with the French army during the Algerian war before embarking on a criminal career. He was on the run from French justice when he arrived in Canada in 1968 with his girlfriend, Jeanne Schneider. The couple got jobs with a handicapped millionaire from Saint-Hilaire, then kidnapped him to get a $200,000 ransom.

Still on the run, Mesrine and Schneider travelled to the Gaspé on two occasions. On their second trip, they robbed and killed an old innkeeper from Percé, Evelyne Le Bouthillier. They then ran off to Texas, where the authorities quickly captured them. Because he was wanted in Quebec only for kidnapping the millionaire, Mesrine declined to contest his expulsion from the United States and was returned to Montreal. He looked like a movie star when police officers escorted him off the plane. Swaggering, cigarette in his mouth, he had the provocative demeanour that became his trademark. He got ten years for the kidnapping, and was taken to Saint-Vincent de Paul Penitentiary, where he was given number 5933.

Mesrine got out of prison to be tried in Montmagny for the murder of the Percé innkeeper. The trial was sensational. It featured surprise witnesses, unexpected revelations, and plenty of courtroom pyrotechnics. It ended with the acquittal of Mesrine and his companion. Judge Paul Miquelon created a stir by admonishing the jurors who acquitted the couple. "I'm bound by your verdict," said the judge, "but I totally disagree with your decision; I hope your conscience lets you sleep soundly." Then, turning to Mesrine and Schneider, he suggested they pray to Mrs. Le Bouthillier for forgiveness.

In prison, Mesrine befriended the toughest inmates, guys like Jean-Paul Mercier, Albert Thibault, and Pierre Vincent. On August 21, 1972, Mesrine and Mercier escaped with four other convicts. The group split up and escapees robbed banks and credit unions to provide for their needs. On September 3, the duo returned to the penitentiary to stage a major attack designed to help their friends escape. Their plan was to organize a massive escape during a field day held for prisoners and their families. The two tough guys were heavily armed, but the plot was foiled when two Laval police officers patrolling in the area spotted the two hooligans behaving in a suspicious manner. They barely managed to escape.

One week later, the Mesrine-Mercier duo was surprised by two game wardens while trying out their weapons on a small isolated road in Saint-Louis-de-Blandford. They shot the two wardens in cold blood. In his book, *L'instinct de mort*, Mesrine explained that they'd fired at wardens Médéric Côté and Ernest Saint-Pierre when the latter recognized them. "It was us or them," he wrote.

The two fled to Venezuela with their companions, where they led the good life for several days. Mercier then returned to Montreal, while Mesrine headed to France.

Both were arrested rather quickly. Mercier later managed another escape, along with Richard Blass, with help from Jocelyne Deraîche, Mesrine's girlfriend. She also had returned to Canada following her boyfriend's capture. Mesrine's exploits then became dazzling. No longer having anything to lose, he committed a string of increasingly daring holdups. Captured once again, he was jailed at la Santé in Paris.

Mesrine always delighted in laughing and scoffing at police officers. He once even showed up at a police station wearing a disguise while he was the most wanted man in America and Europe. Journalists were also his targets. One was attacked and stabbed, another got death threats after writing articles about him. In Canada, Mesrine was a media celebrity. The Montreal lawyer with whom I crossed swords, Raymond Daoust, was an admirer of Mesrine. He decided to launch his own paper to get coverage he felt satisfactory. The weekly *Photo-Police* featured Mesrine's exploits, as did another paper, *Allô-Police*.

On November 2, 1979, Mesrine was shot dead by police in Paris. Officers said they wanted to take no risks, given the number of threats they got from the man who'd become France's public enemy number one. Two grenades were found beside him when they approached to confirm that he was dead.

Richard Blass wasn't of the same calibre as his friend Mesrine, but his style and taste for blood were similar. There were three Blass brothers. One brother, Michel, came into his own later, but the other, Mario, was, let's say, a great deal weaker and less involved than his brothers in the local underworld.

Richard Blass was a minor criminal who enjoyed great notoriety when he and his gang of friends, all French Canadian, set out to eliminate the "Italians," as the media called local Mafia bigwigs at the time. This little ethnic war started in nightclubs, when Blass's friends, who were very turbulent, ran afoul of Vincenzo Di Maulo, who ran le Petit Baril, a bar on Saint-Laurent Boulevard. Blass lost two friends on May 4, 1968, killed at the door of Di Maulo's bar. He and his friend Robert Allard swore to each other that all the Italians would be killed. To prepare their vengeance, they decided to retrieve the bodies of their murdered friends, Gilles Bienvenue and Albert Ouimet. Had the police not intervened in time, they would've executed their plan, which was to replace the bodies of their friends at the funeral home with those of two Mafiosos. The war lasted for some time, with corpses piling up on both sides. One day, after they'd had a drink, Blass and Allard were nabbed by police officers as they were heading to the city's east end to settle accounts with Frank Cotroni.

Though I'd once spoken to Blass on the phone, I saw him for the first time after he'd been shot in a garage on Saint-Michel Boulevard. He'd taken three bullets to the head. Despite his injuries, he managed to bawl out a medic who'd allowed the stretcher he was lying on to roll over to the wall. "You don't have to finish me off, goddammit!" he hollered at the rather dumbfounded young man. Three Italian killers had again missed Blass. He was dubbed "the cat with nine lives," because he survived so many attempts on his life. On October 10, 1968, when he was shot in the garage, it looked as though his luck had run out. However, three weeks later, he was taken to the court to try to identify his aggressors. Blass swore that the three accused men were not the ones who had tried to kill him.

His career lasted less than ten years, but it was very violent and included several armed robberies. The police named Blass as a suspect for twenty murders, fifteen of which were committed in the same place, the Gargantua, a Beaubien Street bar. On October 30, 1974, Blass and his accomplice, Edgar Roussel, with whom he'd just escaped from jail, liquidated two former criminal partners. Blass blamed Roger Lévesque, nicknamed Seven-Up, for denouncing him to the police, and Raymond Laurier for foiling a robbery that had landed Blass in jail for six years. The following January 25, Blass returned to the

Gargantua to murder a witness to some trivial business having to do with arson, and for which his brother Mario had just been charged. He killed the bar manager, Réjean Fortin, to prevent him from testifying, then locked the twelve customers present into a small room where beer cases were stored, and set fire in several spots before escaping. These people met a horrible end.

A few hours following the carnage, I met Mario in front of the nightclub's burnt ruins. He agreed to be photographed and defended his brother, saying the latter had absolutely nothing to do with this awful tragedy. Richard Blass, for his part, didn't contact any journalists, as he sometimes did. He never said a thing about the murder of the manager and twelve customers at the Gargantua.

During his escape, he had pictures taken of himself and accomplice Edgar Roussel in their Longueil hideout, and then one in Rosemont. He sent the photos to André Rufiange, the *Journal de Montréal* columnist, along with humorous letters, in response to questions Rufiange had asked Blass in his column.

Following the Beaubien Street tragedy all of Blass's friends were placed under electronic surveillance. Two young women informed police that the fugitive was plotting an even more spectacular strike than the one at the Gargantua, without giving details about the scheme. Then, on January 23, 1975, Blass's lair in a small Rosemont apartment was finally located. Since the place was hard to surround, and it was known that Blass had a considerable arsenal, police decided to wait.

I learned through a contact that Blass was in the Rosemont building with his girlfriend and another couple. With my photographer friend Pierre McCann, I took up a position a good distance from the building. We saw people leave the building and pile into a car, which the police then followed. A few moments later, I learned that one of these individuals – a little-old lady – who had just left was Blass in disguise.

I informed my colleagues on the night shift, who then drove
off for the Laurentians, to where we knew the police had followed the car. Barely a few hours later, Blass and his friends
were surrounded. A gunfight broke out. While his three companions were somehow ushered from the premises, Blass,
according to the official version, was left alone in his room with
a weapon in hand. Killed with twenty bullets from two different
guns. He was twenty-nine years old.

In the criminal world, certain young people have had brief but
notable careers. This was the case for brothers Jean-Guy and
Roland Giguère of Montreal's east end, who were murdered by
criminals they were competing against.

Jean-Guy Giguère was decidedly adventurous. That's why
he took on "contracts" and committed murders other killers
refused to carry out. Thanks to a go-between, I met Giguère on
a few occasions in one of his favourite places, a restaurant in
Montreal North. He was careful never to compromise himself
when he spoke to me, but he was notably less reticent when dis-
cussing the crimes and activities of other mobsters. He agreed
to meet me on condition I not quote him or say I'd interviewed
him. "Especially don't go saying you had an exclusive interview
with me!" I fully understood his conditions. What I wanted was
information on the crime community from someone completely
conversant with what was going on in that violent little world.

Jean-Guy Giguère was killed on August 23, 1975. That
night, armed guards were present inside the Ontario Street
funeral parlour where he was taken, in the neighbourhood
where the two brothers had grown up. Roland observed that
nothing was too good for his brother. "I've just spent three thousand dollars on flowers and six thousand on the most beautiful

casket," he said. He swore to whoever would listen that he'd avenge Jean-Guy.

A year later, on August 9, 1976, around noon, two hooded gunmen showed up at a Fleury Street brasserie to kill Roland Giguère in his office. They also killed an employee who was trying to thwart their escape. Later on, Donald Lavoie, the Dubois brothers' hired killer, admitted to police that he was one of Giguère's murderers. "He was an informer," was the motive Lavoie invoked to explain the murder.

At the height of the biker war, writing another chapter concerning the life of informers in the crime business, I described these individuals as *canaris*, a term used in French argot. Two of these characters, prisoners in the Parthenais jail, didn't like the description. A phone call sufficed to reassure these gentlemen, who were insulted by use of the word "*canari*," which they'd mistaken for the word "*serin*," used in Quebec to designate a homosexual's little friend.

These imprisoned *canaris* often have time to read newspapers and talk to journalists. That's how I got to have meetings and interesting discussions about the underworld with most of the informers who made headlines in Quebec over the last thirty years. Only one has declined all requests and has never said a word publicly. His name is Yves "Apache" Trudeau, member in good standing of the Hells Angels, who admitted to having committed forty-three murders in fifteen years. He may have committed more, but couldn't remember all his crimes.

Trudeau chose to admit his crimes and testify against his former friends, so his associates decided to have him killed during the 1985 purge of the Hells Angels. A majority of the organization's members had agreed to kill most members of

Laval's North chapter because the latter consumed too many drugs and had become a nuisance. In fact, Trudeau and his friend Michel "Mike" Blass had become money collectors for Allan Ross, called la Belette, or the Weasel, leader of the West End Gang. Their schemes had greatly displeased biker leaders.

Trudeau was in detox when he learned about the plot to kill him. This is what prompted him to become an informer. When I reported that Trudeau became the first Hells Angel to squeal, the news was quickly replayed in all the media and caused a sensation in the milieu. He was the last criminal anyone thought would become a snitch.

Michel Blass also admitted his crimes and became an informer. He was rewarded with a reduced sentence but was again involved in a foul murder shortly after his release. Most informers are quickly forgotten when they leave jail. Trudeau, for his part, got a new identity and vanished. The story is told in well-informed circles that he's so clever at concealing facts that even his new girlfriend knows nothing about his past. Many believe that these people have their faces altered by plastic surgery when they disappear, but, to my knowledge, none of the notorious criminals who testified against their peers underwent such an operation. Some, it is true, are masters at disguising themselves.

This is the case for Réal Simard, the killer who worked for Frank Cotroni, whom I didn't recognize a few years after he was sentenced. He was chatting with police officers from the anti-gang squad, enjoying himself thoroughly at having fooled me. Simard wrote two books based on his experience. Many informers think they'll make a fortune by writing their memoirs or having them written by an experienced journalist. They are most often disappointed. The book market being what it is, few works on crime become best-sellers.

Most informers are criminals who, suddenly finding themselves in dire straits, choose to avoid the worst by disclosing all their secrets. They thereby hand their friends directly over to the police, often losing their companions in the process, who most often come from the same circles they do. Moreover, since they've lived off of crime all their lives, it's very difficult for them to earn an honest living.

Another problem for individuals attempting to start a new life arises from the fact that Quebec isn't really in a position to create a credible history for its informers. The government can provide a new social insurance card and driver's licence, but these characters need an entire history both for themselves and their families, which turns out to be very complicated. For instance, if the criminal wants to go back to school, he has to provide official documents attesting to previous studies. The provincial government can't even issue a new birth certificate to the new citizen the informer is becoming. Many become disillusioned after collaborating for a few months or years.

Others get bored and commit a succession of blunders in prison, where it's difficult for them to assume their new role as collaborators with the law. Such deviations aren't easily forgiven in the prison world. Aimé Simard, nicknamed Ace, was recruited as a hit man by the Hells Angels. He was ungovernable before being sentenced, and has remained so. He must serve at least twelve years of the life sentence given for his string of murders. However, because of his fiery temper, he's served most of his time in solitary confinement, at Port Cartier, in extremely difficult conditions.

Most informers are individuals who have been arrested and who cooperate to get out of prison as fast as possible. A few act out of their own accord, without having been caught red-handed. This was the case for Douglas Jaworski, an airplane

pilot who showed up in the RCMP's office at Toronto's Lester B.
Pearson International Airport to offer his services. Police officers
were incredulous when this polite and well-dressed young man
offered nothing less than an opportunity to trap major players in
the Colombian cocaine cartel. Jaworski, of course, didn't want to
become an informer out of high-mindedness. He was hoping
Canadian authorities, in exchange for his services, could intervene with American justice officials, who were after the twenty-
nine-year-old for money laundering. Jaworski worked for
Colombian traffickers, notably by selling his services for the pur-
chases of planes, and became right-hand man to Diego Caceydo,
a boss with the Medellín cartel. He travelled to Colombia a few
times to prepare for a large delivery. He told his bosses he had
purchased a small and remote landing strip in New Brunswick.
His connivance with the police led to the arrest of some twenty
people, and the seizure, in April 1998, of five hundred kilograms
of pure cocaine with a street value of $200 million. It was the
largest cocaine bust in Canada at the time. Millions of dollars in
cash were also seized. Besides obtaining police protection for his
family and himself, Jaworski pocketed $380,000.

Following a sensational trial where he'd been in the spot-
light, Jaworski gave me his first interview. The young man was
triumphant. But he also recognized that his role in the arrest of
major Colombian traffickers and their henchmen put his life at
risk. "They won't get the satisfaction of seeing me dead," he
told me.

My career has given me the opportunity to rub shoulders with
two very important characters from the famous French drug
connection. This network had long supplied American heroin
consumers, processing the drugs in illicit Marseille labs before
taking them to New York via Montreal.

One of these characters was a police informer of a rarely seen calibre, a bounty hunter named René Quintin de Kercadio, a count from Brittany. The other was Michel Mastantuono, a young cook from Marseille who'd been a lover to Quebec actress Danielle Ouimet while being a drug importer. When caught by the RCMP, he betrayed all his associates, including the woman he lived with in a luxurious Habitat 67 condominium, the famous real-estate complex that has become part of the Montreal landscape.

I got an exclusive interview with the Count de Kercadio at the end of May 1979. This was one of the last feature articles I wrote before leaving *La Presse* for a new career in the electronic media. Heroin and cocaine traffickers had nicknamed Kercadio le Boiteux, or the Hobbler, because he walked with a limp caused by a plane accident during his military service in France. At least that's the explanation he gave to me.

To do the interview, I had to submit to several conditions because Kercadio absolutely wanted to ensure that neither he nor I were followed. He knew he was on the Mafia's blacklist; this wasn't a game but a question of survival. During the interview, which took place in New York, the famous count, who'd got fifty or so of the world's biggest drug traffickers imprisoned, pressed me to help him write his memoirs. I declined, not because his story was uninteresting, far from it, but because I didn't have the means to follow the man even for a few days. He had a regal lifestyle. He frequented only the grandest hotels and the most expensive restaurants. His trademark was a bottle of Dom Perignon champagne. His biography, published in France a few years later, met with a good deal of success.

He lived in Mexico, but had problems with police in France, Canada, and the United States. He said he was unhappy that he hadn't personally managed to nab Frank Cotroni, settling instead for having him caught by four of his immediate assistants. He blamed a private investigator from Montreal for foiling his plan. The P.I., Edwin Pearson, was himself a criminal who'd learned rudiments of the law during his numerous stays in prison. Hired by Conrad Bouchard, the Montreal crime boss in Cotroni's organization and one of the count's targets, Pearson had discovered a photo of Kercadio and Gilles Poissant, a pillar of the RCMP's drug squad in Montreal. Publication of that photo had eliminated all Kercadio's chances of making new captures, in Quebec at least.

The count had tried to earn a living in the underworld, but got arrested the first time he tried to traffic heroin. He was charged in France, where, at the time, fortunately for him, sentences were much lighter than in North America. He got off with two years in the slammer. When he got out, he contacted American police officers in New York to offer his services as a "very special correspondent."

His plan was rather simple. He had contacts among drug traffickers and underworld acquaintances in Canada and the United States. All the police had to do was let him do his trafficking, intervening only when heroin deliveries had been made. His plan worked for ten-odd years, then he was caught trying to trick French and Canadian police. René Quentin de Kercadio wanted to take advantage of his position as informer to transport heroin on the quiet without telling the authorities, thereby making huge profits without taking risks. His plan failed thanks to the presence of another informer in his gang. The police, knowing what to expect with characters like the count, had recruited his own assistant to keep an eye on him.

Despite the failure of this underhanded trick, Kercadio managed to work again after convincing the police of his honesty and repentance. Each year, he'd send me a Christmas card and a bottle of champagne. Then, one year, his present didn't arrive. I later found out that he died in Mexico. For a while, Montreal criminals had thought that the Hobbler had returned to Canada, but this was only a rumour started by those who feared René Quentin de Kercadio like the plague. Was he, in fact, a member of the aristocracy and was his name really Kercadio? I've always asked myself many questions about this fascinating character who could have stepped right out of the pages of a novel.

The other French trafficker was Michel Mastantuono, who confessed in New York, thereby implicating major buyers from the American Mafia and several intermediaries, including certain Quebec entertainers who'd helped him smuggle nearly two hundred kilograms of heroin from Paris to New York via the Port of Montreal.

Even if he'd only been a barman, his arrest would've been big news, but Mastantuono, the barman at the Chez Clairette nightclub, was also the lover of Danielle Ouimet. Ouimet was famous as the first Quebec actress to strip for the camera. The film *Valérie* had caused a scandal in the 1960s because it contained scenes felt to be too daring for the times, though they're very innocent compared to those in X-rated films today.

Mastantuono needed money when he showed up in Montreal. He loved the high life, but his salary working for Clairette wasn't enough to fill his needs. He quickly discovered that two of his French compatriots had easy lives and lots of money. Mastantuono, who'd mixed with criminals since childhood, didn't need a drawing to understand his friends were in the drug business.

Edmond Taillet was a rather popular entertainer in France at the time. He'd taken part in several shows in Montreal in the days when Charles Aznavour and Pierre Roche were the best-known duet in Quebec. Taillet was often at Chez Clairette's with Édouard Rimbaud, author of detective novels popular in

France, written under the pseudonym of Louis Salinas. Both worked for Corsicans from Marseille, Joseph Mari, dubbed le Frisée, or Curly, and Jean-Baptiste Croce.

Ultimately, what the French had set up was an entire network of entertainers. They had smuggled twenty-three kilograms of heroin by concealing them in the amplifiers that had entered Canada with the instruments of Johnny Hallyday's musicians. They also used the services of Jacques Bec, manager of the comedy group called Les Charlots, which was very popular at the time.

Mastantuono organized his part of the network in Montreal. He travelled to France with his fiancée, Danielle Ouimet, giving her money to purchase a Citroën DS21, which was stuffed with forty kilos of heroin. The car was transported to Montreal on a boat and delivered to the New York Mafia by the actress and her boyfriend. As a result of this and three other similar shipments, Mastantuono was responsible for bringing 190 kilos of pure heroin into the United States. He was arrested on October 27, 1971, but never directly implicated his girlfriend in his criminal activities. Condemned to five years in jail, he confessed and revealed the ramifications of his network.

On March 22, 1973, when a series of articles relating the activities of members of the entertainment connection began to be published, a lawyer claiming to represent Ouimet sent a formal demand to *La Presse*, requesting that it stop associating his client with a network of drug traffickers. Claiming that the articles I'd written were "tendentious, false, libellous and defamatory," he threatened to take legal action if information concerning his client continued to be published. He also requested a published retraction. Unfortunately for the actress, none of her attorney's requests were granted, and publication continued.

The actress only acknowledged having belonged to the network in November 1975. Following lengthy negotiations, she admitted to having travelled to Miami to facilitate contacts between two French traffickers who lived at her place in Montreal's Habitat 67 and the heroin buyer linked to the New York Mafia. Ouimet had previously obtained immunity against any future legal action and the promise that her confession of guilt would be submitted to the court as mitigating circumstances.

The actress no longer had any options. American justice absolutely needed her testimony to corroborate that of Mastantuono, who was explaining his meetings with brothers Joseph and Anthony Stassi, who were among the main defendants. I wrote a book on this story in 1976. Entitled *Mastantuono*, it related the story the trafficker had told me. It also included information from official documents submitted to the courts, as well as other information I'd gathered. It remained on Quebec's best-seller list for several weeks.

In March 1976, Danielle Ouimet got off with a suspended sentence and a five-year probation. The New York Mafiosos from the Gambino family who'd bought the drugs got sentences of twenty-five and thirty years, besides fines of $260,000. Michel Mastantuono got a new identity and moved somewhere in the United States. No one's heard about him since.

Between February and September 1976, journalist Jean-Pierre Charbonneau and I worked together on a few organized-crime investigations before Charbonneau definitely gave up journalism for politics. (He is currently Quebec's Minister of Intergovernmental Affairs.)

In 1970, while he was a trainee with *La Presse*, we wrote a long series of articles on Quebec's underworld. Readers never saw them because they were far too theoretical and written by two young and inexperienced journalists. However, a second investigation undertaken at the beginning of 1976 for *La Presse*

represented really solid work. We examined the activities of one
of the kings of the Parisian mob who was trying to invest millions of dollars in Montreal real estate. This was our first mutual
adventure, having for a few years been fierce competitors, with
Charbonneau being my counterpart at *Le Devoir*. Our bosses
thought our reports too risky and tendentious.

However, in the months that followed, French papers and
periodicals widely circulated the information we'd gathered
many months previously. Ironically, in 1991 this saga concerning the French mob was again talked about when a businessman
linked to the Zemmour family tried to buy up the bankrupt
Pascal store chain.

Gilbert Max Zemmour, who had taken refuge in Miami, was
murdered on July 28, 1983. He was the thirty-ninth victim of a
bloody gang war started following internal frictions with his
employees and associates. None of these settlings of accounts led
to any charges. Four of the five Zemmour brothers, born in Sétif,
Algeria, were shot and killed in France, where they had landed
in 1955. Gilbert Max, who had become the family's media
spokesman, always maintained that the Zemmours had been
defamed by police. The story of this criminal family was made
into a film titled *Le Grand Pardon*, starring French actor Roger
Hanin in the role of the Bettoun clan leader. In the film, this
fictitious family carried out the same financial activities as did
the famous Zemmours, or the Z gang as Parisians called them.

This family became known in the protection racket, at first
among Jewish shopkeepers from the du Sentier quarter and the
Montmartre suburb. After some time, the Pied Noir Gang
boasted no fewer than two hundred members, including what
French police have called "second knives" and "third triggers."
In succeeding years, the Z family had made tremendous
headway and broadened its sphere of influence. The brothers
and their henchmen ran various businesses linked to the sex

As a young journalist, I tried to obtain information from Justice Minister Jérôme Choquette, in the midst of the October Crisis.

René Picard, *La Presse*

The Hilton brothers didn't make headlines in boxing alone. The media often reported their problems with the law, especially those of Davey, the eldest.

The infamous Lucien Rivard returns to Canada following several years in a U.S. jail. I got a scoop by driving him home.

My story about the Soviet spy who was on the committee for the 1976 Montreal Olympic Games caused a sensation.

Hells Angels attend the funeral of a fellow member in Trois-Rivières, in June 1997.

Members of the Montreal chapter of the Hells Angels in the mid 1990s.

Veteran Hells Angels carry the casket of a brother buried in 2000.

Yvan Tremblay, *Le Journal de Montréal*

I question three bikers, including Rock Machine president Renaud Jomphe, at a Verdun funeral in October 1995.

Claude Rivest, *Le Journal de Montréal*.

A previously unpublished photo of Maurice "Mom" Boucher, inside the Rockers headquarters on Guilford Street in Montreal.

Ginette Martineau was charged with illegally searching my file at the Société d'assurance automobile du Québec (SAAQ).

Gunsmith Michel Vézina was charged with having made the weapon used in the attempt to kill me.

Thousands of people participated in the march that took place along Mount Royal Avenue, two days following the attempt on my life.

Investigators Jean-François Martin, Michel Whissel, and Guy Bessette are in charge of the investigation into the attack against me.

Jacques Bourdon, *Le Journal de Montréal*

Two journalists who survived attempted murder are reunited when my former collegue Jean-Pierre Charbonneau awards me the National Assembly medal in November 2000.

With Premier Lucien Bouchard, November 2000.

Jacques Bourdon, *Le Journal de Montréal*

With my friend Pierre McCann.

With my two grandchildren, Amélie, born one month following the attempt, and Nicolas.

trade, besides owning nightclubs managed by figureheads. They also got into real-estate dealings. On February 28, 1975, the tides turned on the Zemmour brothers during a gunfight with police at the Le Thélème bar on Saint-Germain Boulevard. A police officer was wounded, while William Zemmour was killed, and his brother Edgar and their uncle William were seriously wounded. A team of police officers from the anti-gang squad had shown up at the bar to interrupt a family meeting. The Zs, however, thought they were being attacked by their enemies.

One week later, Gilbert Max Zemmour, who had just moved to Montreal, was turned back at the border when returning from Miami, where he'd purchased an expensive apartment. Canada was reproaching him for failing to respect the conditions of his temporary residence permit. He'd rented an apartment for three years and had made long-term commitments, including that of bringing his family over, while he was supposed to stay in Canada for only a few months.

Only after this forced expulsion did we get wind of the problems the French mobster was having in Montreal and in his operating base in the red-light districts of Paris and elsewhere in Europe. Gilbert Zemmour and his associates managed to purchase several buildings in Montreal and launch three major construction projects. It was said they had $5 million in the bank and important guarantees from Swiss banks. I made my way to Pine Tree Drive in Miami Beach to try to obtain information and explanations from Zemmour. He refused to be interviewed and there was no way to change his mind.

A French police officer, Commissioner Roger Le Taillanter, wrote following his retirement that the Zemmours had always refused to get involved in the drug trade "out of respect for their children," according to the former boss of the anti-drug squad. In a book published in 1986, *Les Derniers Seigneurs de la pègre* (Last Lords of the Mob), Le Taillanter explained how the Zs had wanted to set up, in Paris, a system similar to the one used by Mafia bosses. They dreamed of reigning as absolute masters over the French underworld. Their appetite was perhaps too voracious, and consequently their enemies and opponents too numerous, for them to succeed.

$$\boxed{6}$$

Strong Competition

E ven when several journalists cover a story, there's nearly always a way to find a different angle. I have made it a rule never to be satisfied unless I have more material than my colleagues. This self-imposed discipline has helped me get genuine satisfaction from doing my job to this day. Press conferences may be the least satisfactory source of information. I cover them anyhow because sometimes I don't have a choice. But I try to do so as seldom as possible.

To some extent, we journalists have been relegated to bit parts by all-news networks. Many organizations wait for RDI[*] producers to give them the signal before they start news conferences. This is when journalists who love to hear or see themselves on television start asking insipid questions. Personally I mostly avoid asking questions.

On rare occasions, however, press conferences can be useful. I got an exclusive once, when the RCMP was briefing the

---

[*] RDI is the CBC's French-language all-news network, the Réseau de l'information.

press on a major drug raid in Nova Scotia. The officer giving
details about the police operation briefly mentioned infiltration.
No other journalist picked up on this detail. Standing at a distance from my colleagues, I discreetly asked the right questions
and discovered that one of the traffickers' right-hand men was
working for the police. He'd become a source agent, which in
police language refers to a criminal who'll eventually testify. The
day following this press conference in Montreal, my article was
circulated on the press wire and made headlines elsewhere in
the country.

I again got a leg up on my colleagues in September 1975.
This was in an era before police squads routinely employed
public-relations people to keep journalists fully informed of
their doings: we still had to work to get a story. During a major
operation, the RCMP finally gave in to repeated requests from
journalists covering the Montreal drug squad's investigations.
Frank Roach from the CBC, Jean-Pierre Charbonneau from *Le
Devoir*, and I from *La Presse* were invited to follow the final
hours of a major investigation.

Operation Zapata had been going on for months. Investigators had travelled to Spain and Morocco, following traffickers
who were getting ready to import seven hundred kilos of hashish,
a large quantity at the time. The investigation was wrapped up
even before the drugs reached the Port of Montreal. Police had
gathered enough evidence to charge twenty-five people, including a school principal, a provincial official, and a QPF officer
who'd acted as a countersurveillance specialist. He was supposed to determine whether police were tailing the traffickers.

So we followed police surveillance operations from the Port
of Montreal. What was supposed to take a few hours lasted two
days, prompting our television colleague to let a cameraman
take his place. I remember Charbonneau's complaints about the
time it was taking for the investigation to wrap up. The more the

hours past, the less time he had to write his article – the deadline at *Le Devoir* being around 9 P.M. Pressed for time, he settled for reporting the official version of the police raid, while I carefully described how officers had tailed the traffickers, and how they had bugged the recreational vehicle in whose walls and gas tank the drugs had been stashed.

This was one of the few times police agreed to include journalists in a major investigation, giving us what amounted to ringside seats. I decided to follow the team that had been posted behind the small Saint-Eustache warehouse, where the traffickers had set up their headquarters.

The traffickers had said they'd open a bottle of champagne when the first drug bag was pulled from its hiding place. Thanks to the microphone, we heard them struggle for nearly two hours trying to remove the tank from under the vehicle. Then, suddenly, police heard the sound of a popping cork. It was the appointed moment to nab the crooks. Before they had even put up their hands, I had snapped a few pictures.

Criminals aren't the only ones put in jail. Journalists can get a taste of that medicine as well, which is what happened to me in Palermo, Sicily, in May 1996. My crime: I'd taken photos of the exterior of the Ucciardone prison, an eight-hundred-year-old building at the centre of the island's capital. Fortunately, I was able to save my negative. This is a question of principle for a journalist: absolutely no one should tell him what photo he can or can't take. In Italy, several authorizations are apparently needed to photograph state properties or even officials.

I didn't realize the commotion I'd created among guards at the doors of the imposing prison or among the numerous soldiers stationed on the sidewalks. I entered the church on the other side of the street, right in front of the huge prison's main door. The priest greeted me with open arms. Though Italians are reputedly loquacious, this was especially true of Father Paolo Turturo. He told me he was cousin to actor John Turturo, famous both in Italy and the United States. The priest, a former boxer who was fifty years old at the time, had plenty of nerve. He'd organize demonstrations with children in front of the church to denounce the Mafia, which prompted someone to place a bomb at the door of his sacristy.

The good priest didn't hesitate to help me when a young parishioner came over to tell him that soldiers were surrounding the church and awaiting a photographer at its door. Father Turturo asked if I'd taken photos of the soldiers or prison. He invited me to leave the negative with him. I then placed a blank film in the camera. When I left the church, soldiers were waiting to take me to the prison warden. I found this rather amusing, unlike my driver-interpreter, who was left standing on the sidewalk.

On the inside, guards were having fun dealing with me. My rough Italian and their shaky French or English made for delightful conversation. Ironically, I'd taken steps to visit this prison and especially the two Montreal criminals in it. I waited two hours for a report to be made on my film – which was blank. Two hours that allowed me to get a glimpse of prison life from the guards' quarters and to witness the comings and goings of prisoners and their visitors. A prison is a prison, even if built in the eleventh century. Walls define a prisoner's life, whether he is in Bordeaux, Saint-Vincent de Paul, or Donnacona.

My trip to Sicily put me on the trail of criminal organizations that are active in Canada. I met Italian police officers and judges who were just beginning to make major inroads against the criminal octopus. Since then, dozens of notorious criminals have become *pentiti*, penitents, or *balances* as they're called in France. In Canada, they're simply referred to as informers. During this investigation on Mafia activities between Sicily and Montreal, I obtained a lot of new information on members of the Caruana and Cuntrera families, a quasi-independent group that had risen to the forefront of international drug trafficking and money laundering. Alfonso Caruana, head of the clan, was wanted everywhere in the world after being sentenced in Palermo.

He was later jailed with his brothers while trying to resume his trafficking activities between Montreal, Toronto, Mexico, and Venezuela. The Caruana-Cuntrera families are still intimately linked to that of Nicolo Rizzuto, Canada's boss of bosses, who oversees the activities of "men of honour" here.

I was able to question Caruana a few months later. He'd been called before a judge in Montreal, and I followed him through the hallway to the elevator, asking him a long series of questions. The Mafioso never flinched but remained impassive and said not a word. He didn't even seem annoyed when my questions were deliberately provocative. Later, when officers with Toronto's special organized-crime squad set up Project Omerta to try to catch him, they observed that the meaning of the word "*omerta*," or secret oath, fully applied to Alfonso Caruana.

A year after my lengthy investigation of Sicily's Mafia, I headed to Asia to complete this report on international drug trafficking. I met a few Canadians living in the hell of Thai prisons and, in Pakistan, police officers posted with a United Nations' agency. I also witnessed the horror of the civil war in Afghanistan up close.

Alain Olivier was a heroin consumer who'd travelled to Thailand to do runs for a Quebec heroin trafficker. This was trade on a small scale, partly helping the individuals involved to make a living and pay for their drugs, which were very expensive over here. It wasn't unusual at the time for consumers to travel to Asia and, using very plain envelopes, send a few ounces of heroin to their Canadian addresses, via the Royal Mail. The

Canadian law facilitated their task since customs officers and police weren't allowed to open first-class mail.

Olivier, a young man from Drummondville, ran out of luck on his last trip to the east. He ended up having to beg for drugs in a city in northern Thailand. He managed to find only a kilo for his buyer, who was in fact a secret agent with the RCMP's Vancouver drug squad. The transaction turned into a tragedy. The drug buyer and seller started to quarrel in the box of a pickup truck. When police intervened, the driver accelerated flat out, throwing the Canadian secret agent onto the pavement, killing him on the spot.

In prison, Olivier claimed that the police officer was killed by a gunshot from one of his colleagues. This changed nothing, however, since capital punishment is what he had in store after his arrest. His sentence was commuted to life imprisonment. It was a bitter and disgruntled individual that I met in the Bangkwang prison's visitors' quarters. A magnificent garden of flowers and shrubs lay next to the cells where prisoners were taken to meet visitors. The only beautiful place in this huge prison, according to Olivier. Through two grills, the Quebecer told me about the difficulties of prison life, saying Canadian jails were luxury hotels compared with the one in Bangkwang. He didn't even have a bed and had to sleep on the floor. Following eight years of imprisonment, the young man was disgusted with the cops who'd drawn him into a trap.

His Quebec cronies, as guilty as he was and even more so, had long ago been paroled. But he'd still have to wait several months before being transferred to Canada to finish his sentence, thanks to a prisoner-exchange program. In fact, he was almost immediately transferred to a halfway house, then released on probation.

In Peshawar, Pakistan, I also came across Rehmat Shaw Afridi, the major hashish supplier to Montreal's large criminal organizations. Besides being a drug supplier, he was also editor of *The Frontier Post*, the area's leading newspaper. This town, located along the world's most dangerous border, where anything can be bought, from canons to handguns, boasts the riskiest market in the entire region. Afridi refused to see me. However, he regularly spoke to major drug importers from Montreal. His name is still on the list of the accused in at least two drug importing deals that await proceedings in Montreal's provincial court.

This Asian investigation allowed me to travel to the most dangerous corners of Thailand. I even visited a brothel, which I described in great detail to my readers. The only thing I consumed there, however, was a beer. After reading my article, one of my friends said, "Either you're an idiot or a damned liar!" I'd written nothing but the truth.

| 7 |

Television Moments

Though I've always preferred written journalism, working with television colleagues has occasionally given me a lot of pleasure. I drew a great deal of satisfaction from being a part of the CBC's *the fifth estate* team for five years.

My first television experience came in 1975, when the CBC's Les Neremberg and Brian McKenna asked me to help them do research for a documentary following the death of Richard Blass. The goal was to find the Quebec desperado's schoolmates and show the difference between those who had led a criminal life and those who became useful citizens. But the research was difficult since most of the people who'd known Blass at an early age were either in jail or had died violently. There were, of course, the crook's next of kin who agreed to talk about him, but the other rare individuals who'd known him refused to appear on TV.

Given the obstacles, the producers decided to shift their focus. So the report on Blass became a series of three one-hour programs on disorganized crime, poorly organized crime, and, finally, organized crime. For the first time in Canada, a TV crew would film criminals without their knowledge. Our project was ambitious: we wanted to track the one and only big boss of the Canadian Mafia, Vincent Cotroni.

We thought that tailing major Mafiosos would be complicated, but the reality was rather amusing. Our work couldn't have been easier. In fact, Mr. Vic, as some called him, had poor eyesight, which made him very cautious at the wheel of his late-model Cadillac. So it was almost child's play to follow and film him with a camera hidden in a plain pickup. That's how we were able to film some of the big boss's meetings with his associates.

For the program on Blass, we brought together friends of the young Montrealer, who agreed to give an alternate view of the criminal's character. One of the interviews was filmed in a Saint-Catherine Street nightclub that was empty at the time. The famous Club 281 has since become a fashionable spot for women travelling to Montreal. It was the first bar featuring male strippers in Canada. As for our program, entitled "Settling Accounts," it earned our team the Anik Prize for best documentary aired on the CBC in 1975.

Two years later, a team of Toronto producers called on me to help with a series of documentaries on organized crime in Canada. This was the second CBC series to be called *Connections*. In 1976, a first such investigation had caused a sensation when it aired, and, with the ambitious resumption of the project, the series would break ratings records.

I followed the trail of Canada's major criminals for over a year with producers William Macadam and Martyn Burke and my research colleague, James Dubro. We also invented new methods to demonstrate the presence of organized crime in Canada, a presence many politicians didn't want to believe in. "There is no mob in Ontario," the province's then-solicitor general, Allan Lawrence, often said.

The team worked amid the greatest secrecy in rented offices

outside the CBC's headquarters. The project had the code name "Commerce." However, the businesses we were examining were rather strange. We did hundreds of interviews and shot thirty thousand metres of film, which is to say fifty hours of footage, throughout Canada, the United States, and Europe.

We hired a former criminal named Frank Angelo to set up a secret operation. Our man would sell stolen bonds to underworld bigwigs, while our crew filmed the scene in a Vancouver hotel. We also exposed the mob's protection and fraud rackets. Obviously, Montreal was at the centre of many of these reports. One in particular showed how a gang of young bikers, who'd recently linked up with the Hells Angels, was poised to eliminate all competition in the Montreal area. (More on this later.)

At about this time, I also met Georges Lemay, one of Canada's best-known criminals. Today, Lemay is retired and collects stamps. Like me, he was born in Shawinigan. Back then, however, he was very active in Montreal's crime world, setting up a lab for making angel dust, a highly dangerous chemical drug. For three months, RCMP officers kept Lemay under constant surveillance. At the time, I got in touch with the famous Montrealer to talk about his most spectacular heist, the robbing of a bank vault.

On July 1, 1961, leading a gang of clever thieves, Lemay robbed the safes of the Bank of Nova Scotia on Saint-Catherine Street, making off with jewellery, extremely valuable documents, and a fortune in cash. The robbery officially yielded $28,000 to its perpetrators, but it is doubtful that anyone was ever able to assess its true value. Some said that it might have amounted to as much as $5 million. Rumour had it that several industrialists doing business in that neighbourhood kept a great deal of cash there, hidden from the tax man's inquisitive gaze.

Lemay was toying with my questions. Though he was always ready to talk, he knew how to stop without having said a thing.

He'd been sentenced for the robbery and had served his time. I first made contact with him in prison, when he'd agreed to give me an interview about the robbery. A born storyteller, he confided that only one box had been left intact, and that the robbers had discovered women's underwear in one of the safes, along with valuables. They'd taken the money, leaving the pink panties behind.

It was only five years later that Lemay was spotted living in Fort Lauderdale, Florida, with his new wife and child aboard a luxurious yacht. Police finally collared him after his photograph had been circulated, thanks to the first transmission of images via the Early Bird satellite.

Lemay's audacity and ostentation have always been astonishing. His first wife was Huguette Daoust, the criminal lawyer's sister. In 1952, Lemay had all police forces in Florida looking for him concerning Huguette's mysterious disappearance, near Tom Harbor, in the southern part of the state. He went into hiding but stayed in the same region. They never proved anything. According to Lemay, Huguette had gone to get clothes in the car while he was on a wharf. She was never seen again.

Lemay joked with me some thirty years later, saying that sharks easily got into certain habits. "If you feed them raw meat one day, they'll be waiting for you the next day, same place, same time," he said with a smile. "Is there a link between this and your wife's disappearance?" I asked. "Of course not!" he answered, still smiling.

He was jailed in the Dade County prison following his arrest on May 6, 1965. He soon escaped. Published reports claimed that he lowered himself to the ground with a telephone cable from a seventh-floor window. However, during our conversations, Lemay said that payment of a large sum of money allowed him to leave the prison through the front door. He and his wife were finally arrested on August 19, 1966, in Las Vegas.

Following a spectacular trial in 1969, Lemay got eight years in prison for robbing 377 safety-deposit boxes. Though later charged with murder, he was acquitted. He afterwards got an eight-year jail sentence for operating a drug lab. I last saw him when he was arrested over this lab, located in Rivières-des-Prairies. He'd briefly lost his smile and even tried to hide his face with his hands. This manoeuvre yielded a great photo for Robert Nadon, my colleague with *La Presse*. Lemay answered a few questions I put to him while I was seated in the police car beside him.

Lemay only learned much later how the police had trapped him. By pure coincidence, he had installed his lab right across the street from a business owned by the Mafia's Violi brothers. A Montreal police surveillance team discovered Lemay on 4th Avenue totally by accident, while watching the comings and goings of an Italian criminal related to the Violis. This character had been involved in the notorious kidnapping of the grandson of American billionaire J. Paul Getty. Kidnappers had demanded a ransom of several million dollars and, to show they were serious, had sent one of their hostage's ears to his family. Lemay should've chosen a more discreet location to set up his phials.

In 1979, I decided to experience new things and put my career on a different path. Following the one-year *Connections* assignment in Toronto, *La Presse*'s newsroom seemed dull. The team was having trouble getting over the eight-month strike, and management didn't like how the dispute had been settled. The company was offering severance packages to all those who wanted to leave. I had two days to decide. I was thirty-five years old and felt I had to consider other prospects. At the time, I thought I could turn one of my hobbies into a job, so I became a farmer in Saint-Cuthbert, near Berthierville. I hoped my passion for bees could provide a living and that I could take advantage of long winter months to dedicate myself to a new career as a freelance journalist.

Things went otherwise. My beekeeping experience lasted only five years, time enough for me to realize that Quebec had no market for commercial apiculture. I became president of beekeepers in my region and secretary of the Quebec Federation of Beekeepers, which gave me the opportunity to meet remarkable people throughout the province.

I've kept very good memories of this time and the hard physical work I did. A journalist always works in the abstract. One day's newspaper is only good for recycling the next. Beekeeping is a solitary profession. It gives you time to think. Working in hives requires great attention to detail. Summer days are never long enough to do all tasks needed to ensure that hives are as productive as possible. Harvest time is very brief and hives must be at full strength for the yield to be profitable.

A beekeeper must walk from one apiary to the next in the countryside, since fields are now used for intensive farming that leaves little room for wildflowers. Strong organizational skills are needed, and beekeeping, like journalism, requires good observation skills. Moreover, there are risks just as there are in journalism. Rummaging through hives bothers bees, which react by stinging intruders.

Some say that bee venom is excellent medication against arthritis. If that's the case, I must be completely immunized, given the thousands of bee stings I've had. My life as a beekeeper was a nice dream, but the reality was very demanding. While going through this experience, I quickly returned to my first passion, journalism.

The day following the announcement I'd be leaving *La Presse*, I got an offer from my colleague Brian McKenna, who'd become producer of *the fifth estate* in Toronto. He asked me if I could dedicate a few weeks to a research project concerning some corruption business. I immediately accepted, and this six-week contract was extended for five wonderful years.

The CBC's public-affairs program is the oldest of its kind in the world. The American CBS network modelled its famous *60 Minutes* on it. My bosses Robin Taylor and Ron Haggart were professionals. Haggart was one of those old journalists with a good nose, able to initiate complicated projects and see them through successfully. Taylor, for his part, was captain of this crew made up of various talents. The team was based in Toronto, while McKenna and I worked in Montreal. Anton Koschany, who later became the boss at *W-5*, the current-affairs program on the competing CTV network, was based in Vancouver.

I worked with Adrienne Clarkson at the time. Though she's now Canada's Governor General, we simply called her Adrienne back then. She worked hard and knew how to create a good atmosphere among her colleagues. When I joined, the program had three hosts, the two others being Eric Malling and Ian Parker. *The fifth estate* usually had three segments, with hosts constantly having projects on the go with different producers or associate producers. The team would prepare and discuss the content of files. Hosts did major interviews, but producers often carried out some of the report on their own. Accordingly, part of the team could be at the other end of the planet while we worked on two or three different files.

As associate producer, I did research and interviews, and planned upcoming shootings. The first real file I worked on concerned research begun, though not completed, by Quebec's Commission of Inquiry into Organized Crime (CIOC). Commissioners had learned that individuals linked to organized crime had easy access to managers of Quebec's liquor commission. As a result, they were able to get favours, place certain products on shelves, and grease their palms in large construction projects. The CIOC also learned that most large distilleries used a political contribution system based on a percentage of their sales in Quebec and in most Canadian provinces.

Though the CIOC had given its report to the Quebec government, the then solicitor general, Fernand Lalonde, had refused to release its contents. I'd obtained a copy of the famous document and written a series of articles on it for *La Presse* in December 1975. But politicians hadn't followed up on the discoveries of the commission, which had said that, by linking their contributions to political party war chests, state suppliers had committed something comparable to extortion.

The fifth estate team agreed to search through court files around the country, wherever police had carried out CIOC investigations with a view to laying charges. I then personally sifted through court files in Quebec and Ontario, provinces where searches had taken place. I discovered a mine of information in reports police had made to the judge who'd issued the search warrant. Detectives had drawn up a detailed list of the cheques they'd found during their search of most of the distilleries doing business with the state-owned companies controlling liquor sales in the provinces. Written on them were the names of those to whom they were made out to and the amounts contributed to campaign funds. The party in power received the lion's share of contributions, but those in opposition weren't forgotten, though they got far less money.

Like accountants, we added and compared amounts given to various political parties. We ran into a major problem in Halifax, where court employees refused to give us access to public documents. After insisting with officials and asking the judge who signed the warrants to intervene, I was still denied access. I then called on the CBC's legal services in Toronto, where the legal problems created by our group of inveterate snoopers kept lawyer Danny Henry busy almost full-time. But the experienced lawyer got no further than I had. We agreed that a CBC journalist from Halifax and a lawyer would repeat the steps I had taken. If need be, we wanted to take this case to the courts and were ready to go all the way. We were right in wanting to be well prepared, since the case went to the Supreme Court, which ruled in our favour on all counts.

This appeal to the Supreme Court was also one of the disappointments of my career. Though I was behind this challenge, the court's official decision, which still stands as a precedent, is called the McIntyre Decision, after Linden McIntyre, who'd undertaken official procedures after I had. Linden, who already had a distinguished career, later became a host of *the fifth estate*. Unfortunately, our show had already aired by the time the court allowed contents of the search warrants to be made public. However, all major media outlets took up and carried on the research we'd started so diligently.

For one part of this report, we travelled to Philadelphia, Pennsylvania, where a state-owned company did business with Canadian firms. To avoid answering questions from the host, one of the American officials started to run, which makes for good TV but not for a very good image of the fugitive.

Some issues never make it to the screen, while others take months before emerging. I spent nearly two years setting up an interview with a hit man. It took months to get Donald Lavoie to sit before a camera, but the interview he gave Hana Gartner was a television first.

This was indeed the first time a hired killer related and admitted to murders in front of millions of viewers. The program segment, titled "Hitman," was enormously successful. Lavoie was frank and very direct in his answers. Gartner didn't spare the killer. She asked very incisive questions, but Lavoie knew how to defend himself, even on camera. Unlike many criminals, he hadn't asked for any special treatment. He was facing the camera. Following one question he thought was too bold, he ordered that everything be stopped, in a tone allowing no other option, but the interview continued afterwards until the host had asked all her questions.

Lavoie had agreed to testify against his former friends from the Dubois clan in the Saint-Henri neighbourhood. Police officers in charge of his file had also agreed to be interviewed for the program. Richard McGinnis, the inspector handling Lavoie's case, and Det.-Capt. Julien Giguère, head of Montreal's anti-gang squad, both maintained that the killer had really changed his life. "We can't forget the horrors committed by this criminal, but a man can change," McGinnis said. He was right since, nearly twenty years later, Lavoie doesn't seem to have reverted to crime. Rumour has it he now leads a quiet life. Police absolutely don't want to disclose his whereabouts. During the interview, Lavoie said he was targeted. "I'm a dead man," he told Gartner. "I'm waiting for a bullet to hit me. I'd like to see that death coming," he added, "but I know I won't see a thing." Life seems to have proven him wrong since he's still alive.

As a journalist with the written press, I nearly always work alone, or at most with the assistance of a photographer. My best experience with team work came when I did television.

I'd just joined *the fifth estate* when one of my contacts told me the RCMP had been investigating the activities of two senior Pakistani officials since the summer. The story had international ramifications, since it involved foreign intelligence services, the British MI-5 and the American CIA.

I learned that the RCMP's security services were handling the Canadian part of this file. This was before the creation of the civilian agency now known as the Canadian Security Intelligence Service (CSIS). For two weeks, between July 7 and 21, 1980, the RCMP's secret agents tailed the two Pakistani officials, Anwar Ali and I. A. Bhatty. The pair were ostensibly travelling to Montreal to do consular work in the Pakistani delegation. Surveillance revealed, however, that the two men had never set foot in the local consulate. RCMP agents knew what the visitors had come here to do, having obtained information from abroad, from secret recordings of conversations between the two diplomats, as well as from their own surveillance and investigation. As they'd done elsewhere around the world, the two officials were discreetly buying parts needed to set up their country's military nuclear program and build the Islamic bomb.

This information was journalistic dynamite (so to speak). I was nearly sure that no other journalist could get the police secrets I had. We therefore would have all the time we needed to prepare a major report. I remember that my colleague, Brian McKenna, was overjoyed when I returned from a top-secret meeting with one of my informers. We immediately put the big machine into gear. Ron Haggart, also jumping for joy, assigned Eric Malling as host. The three of us then pooled our knowledge and resources. We asked for assistance from Virginia Nelson, an expert researcher working in Toronto, and retained the services of Vera Murray, a Canadian journalist working in France and following her husband, CBC foreign correspondent Don Murray. This is how we were able to build a large file based on information published in international papers. We also learned that the BBC had produced a major report on the ambitious Pakistani project a few months earlier.

Pakistan's former prime minister, Ali Bhutto, had once written that his country was ready to do anything, even starve, to build the atomic bomb. "If there is a Hindu bomb, a Jewish bomb, a Christian bomb, a Communist bomb, then why not an

Islamic bomb?" Col. Moammar Gadhafi's Libya was also seriously toying with the idea. At the time, many thought that Gadhafi was secretly funding Pakistan's research, since that country was too poor to shoulder all the costs of building the first nuclear bomb in the Islamic world. Gadhafi was probably right in thinking Israeli secret services would never allow him to complete this kind of research in Libya.

The man heading Pakistan's nuclear bomb project was Dr. Abdul Qadar Khan, a scientist who had been expelled from the Netherlands. He was a brilliant metallurgist, charming, intelligent, liked by his colleagues and neighbours. This scientist had copied, for himself and his country, secret information from the laboratory where he worked, inside the gas treatment factory in Almelo, near Amsterdam. Enriched uranium was produced there, for use in various nuclear installations around the world. Abdul Qadar Khan had worked only seventeen days in Almelo but left with extremely valuable information, including a list of major foreign suppliers. Once back in Islamabad, he created a service whose mission was to travel the world to buy parts for making the gas centrifuges crucial to developing the bomb. The two Pakistani diplomats who had travelled to Montreal were in fact employees of Abdul Qadar Khan.

Canada had already been hoodwinked by India, which had exploded its own atomic bomb on May 18, 1974, using Canadian technology provided with a CANDU reactor, a device intended only for civilian purposes. Moreover, the five countries that had purchased Canadian reactors to produce electricity were also the ones then suspected of having entered a race for atomic weapons. Perhaps this was only a coincidence. They were India, Pakistan, Argentina, South Korea, and Taiwan.

The official affair began at Mirabel airport outside Montreal on August 29, 1980, when Canadian authorities seized a shipment of electronic parts addressed to Tech Equipment, a company in Islamabad. The whole load had a declared value of $56,000. The RCMP and customs officers were acting under the terms of the Customs and Excise Act, which prohibits exporting electronic parts such as military equipment or atomic components from Canada without a permit.

We were relieved because the indictment passed completely unnoticed in the media. It was significant that the secret service had transferred the file to the RCMP's criminal investigations section, because this meant that charges would be laid, which is rather unusual when the country's security is at stake. Such matters are often settled at the diplomatic level. All it takes is the expulsion of one or two diplomats and the file is shelved. Not this time, however, since Canada considered the sale of electronic equipment that could be used to build an atomic bomb far too serious to be quietly filed away.

The fifth estate went into action following this seizure. At first, we followed and filmed all the individuals involved with the shipment. We then carried out a second series of surveillances. This time, our friend Malling, equipped with a microphone hidden under his shirt, asked precise questions to the three people accused of shipping the parts. He got polite answers, but all three emphasized that there was nothing illegal or compromising in their actions. They also said that the parts they had bought were used to build inverters, which are electric current regulators used in the textile industry. One of the shippers, a Saint-Laurent businessman, was particularly talkative. Malling met him a few times and had several phone conversations with him in which he requested a full interview before the cameras. Another individual, an engineer working for a Canadian government agency, was always very polite but said that he'd only give an interview for the purpose of legal proceedings.

We were well prepared to interview this man, a Pakistani immigrant who'd become a Canadian citizen, if he had agreed.

The day of the Mirabel seizure, police had searched his apartment. The next day, he went to the central train station, removed papers and documents from locker number 262, and then threw some of the documents into a garbage can. These documents were later used as evidence against him and his associates at their trial.

Malling's encounter with the engineer was an exploit in itself. We accosted the man as he left his home, an apartment near McGill University, in downtown Montreal. We hadn't expected that the weather would be so lousy that November morning. Nearly a centimetre of ice covered sidewalks and vehicles as Malling, walking beside the scientist, tried to coax information out of him. The engineer remained calm but simply repeated the same phrase: "No comment for now. I'll speak later." He didn't want to say anything about the papers discarded at the central train station, nor explain why he had placed them in a locker there in the first place.

Cameraman Bill Casey filmed the entire scene, which lasted several minutes, while walking backwards on very unstable ground. Malling, however, fell down. The defendant, a dignified man, stopped to help him get up. A few steps farther, our recalcitrant subject slipped and fell and Malling assisted him to his feet. Both laughed at the irony of the situation. But it wasn't over: when he got to his vehicle, the engineer had to scrape the ice off his windows and Malling continued to barrage him with questions.

Brian McKenna, who went to Paris to cover another story, took the opportunity to shoot footage and carry on the research in France. He also made a quick visit to London, where an interview had been scheduled with Anthony Wedgewood-Ben, a former British energy minister, who was revealing that his government had also forbidden the shipment of inverters, since they were no doubt going to be used to build the Pakistani bomb. The sale without permit of all components for these devices had also been forbidden.

To complete our research and get answers from Pakistani representatives, we requested an interview with Ambassador Eltaf A. Sheikh. The interview took place at Pakistan's embassy in Ottawa, on December 2, 1980, in late afternoon, a few hours before our first report aired. We knew this item would make a big splash and had decided to do the interview before the broadcast, knowing it would be difficult to get it afterwards.

I was the one who dealt with the press attaché at the Pakistani embassy. There is a journalistic rule that I've always strictly observed that you must neither lie nor use a false identity when conducting your research. However, this doesn't mean you must tell all the truth at the same time – so I requested an interview with the ambassador concerning trade between our countries. We had also deliberately chosen a rather vague working title for our program to avoid attracting attention: "Import-Export." But Malling and McKenna, once set up inside the ambassador's office, showed their hand at the start of the interview. Disagreeably surprised, the man then defended his country's diplomats, claiming no one had done anything illegal. He also defended the actions of the three Canadians involved in the transactions. After several minutes of responding to Malling's incisive questions, the ambassador had had enough, saying he wanted to end the interview. He accused our team of violating international rules, and said, "I have nothing more to say." He then concluded in a peremptory tone: "Gentlemen, you can leave."

The program created a sensation. Questions were asked in the House of Commons. The day following the first show's broadcast, the federal minister of justice replaced the initial charge with twenty-eight new counts of indictment, eleven of which were related to the export of electronic parts classified as atomic equipment and whose export from Canada is prohibited without a permit. Fourteen other charges were related to importing electronic components from the United States and shipping them to Pakistan, still without appropriate permits. The accused were liable to fines of up to $25,000 and to prison sentences of a maximum of five years. Quebec's present public security minister, Serge Ménard, then a criminal lawyer, defended certain members of the trio, and the case went all the way to the Supreme Court. The file was closed a few years later with a verdict of guilty on only one of the initial twenty-eight charges. The three men were fined.

The trio had also filed a civil suit asking for $75,000 in damages from the CBC. I didn't hear about the case again until 1994, when the Crown corporation's lawyer filed a request to have procedures dismissed since, in one case, nothing had moved in thirteen years. The request was denied. In 1996, a lawyer for the three defendants undertook to revive the old civil suit. Since I was behind these reports, I was questioned at length. It's incredible how you can forget certain important facts and remember details that are almost trivial. However, having viewed the programs again and read various documents, I was able to remember important facts rather well.

On May 28, 1998, Pakistan exploded its first atomic bomb.

This file has since gone back into oblivion.

In 1992, I accepted an invitation from the producer of the TVA network to become the third host of its *911* program dealing with police activities. This was a new challenge and something I could do besides my other work as a journalist. I had a little experience behind the camera, but had never been a TV reporter. Obviously, there was a big difference between my new role and the numerous interviews I'd given to colleagues with the electronic media throughout my career. Gaétan Girouard and Benoît Johnson were the two pillars of this program that had been on the air for a few years. Both were young, but they had acquired vast television experience. Johnson was meticulous and his editing had a precision nothing short of military. As for Girouard, he was a tireless worker and always wanted to attend important events. He toiled away at all hours of the day and night. I dusted off a few old files, as requested by the team, and learned a new side of this profession. This experience allowed me to discover something about television celebrity. One night, when I'd just finished editing a report, I was intercepted on Christophe-Colomb Street by an MUC police cruiser. While one officer filled out a report concerning a defective headlight, the other one, having recognized me, started asking questions about my television work. I didn't get a ticket, but like any other citizen in similar circumstances, I received a forty-eight-hour notice to have repairs done.

I got an exclusive for this program. An airplane stuffed with cocaine had just been seized in Casey, a town in Quebec's upper Mauricie region, and I was invited to attend the destruction of the complete cargo – 4,323 kilograms of cocaine. I witnessed this event with two colleagues: photographer Gilles Lafrance and a cameraman from the *911* program. My bosses at the *Journal de Montréal* allow us to cooperate with other press agencies on condition the information provided to readers isn't affected. The drug traffickers would have surely cried their eyes out had they seen what was happening to the 152 large bundles of cocaine.

A billion dollars in drugs were on this plane from Colombia, which had been detected thanks to a program involving police and military forces from several countries. Seven individuals were sentenced, including the pilot Raymond "Cowboy" Boulanger. The police thought that several criminal organizations had cooperated to share the risks entailed in making this shipment. Despite the huge seizure, the price of cocaine in Quebec bars didn't even go up by a dollar, which proves the supply is plentiful.

The destruction of the cocaine took place under high security at a garbage incinerator on des Carrières Street in Montreal. It took nine people five days to complete the procedure. Officers threw the drugs in two large garbage chutes leading to the fire that burned at very high temperature. No odour could be smelled outside. However, I breathed in a strong dust of this famous powder when I walked between the two garbage chutes. This brief inhalation had a startling effect on me.

A few years later, I questioned the pilot Boulanger, who, once paroled, travelled to Colombia, contrary to the conditions of his release. He was again deported to Canada, which had issued a warrant for his arrest. Back in prison, the Leclerc Institute in Laval, Boulanger swore he hadn't resumed trafficking cocaine. He said he'd explored new air routes to transport vegetables from Colombia to Venezuela. I wrote what he told me, while clearly telling readers I remained skeptical. My doubts were justified. Shortly thereafter I learned about certain documents Boulanger had when he was arrested in South America. He had maps showing safe air routes and remote landing strips in the Gaspé and along the north shore of the Saint Lawrence. Quite a detour for a trip between Colombia and Venezuela.

This kind of exclusive by a journalist usually makes his colleagues angry with the authorities who are his sources. The destruction of drugs from Casey two weeks following their seizure didn't fail to create a stir in the small community of journalists specialized in covering police and legal activities. A few years later, the RCMP's public-relations service explained to members of the force's Quebec division, in its internal newsletter, the *Pony Express*, that opposite effects are produced when a press agency is given an exclusive. They used one of my scoops to demonstrate why other journalists had been upset.

$$8$$

Several Explosive Issues

My knowledge of sports used to be very limited. As children, my brother Gaston and I had been photographed with Jacques Plante, the famous goaltender from Shawinigan who'd also been a classmate of my uncle Gaétan Philibert. As well, the second husband of my father's sister was Arthur Béliveau. Although this didn't make Jean Béliveau my cousin, it did allow me to get a few pucks from the Montreal Forum.

In the early 1980s, I obtained police documents referring to the Mafia infiltration of professional boxing. Like everyone, I'd heard about the exploits of the Hilton brothers, but had no idea what impact this news would have. No one wanted to tell their story on camera, however, so the issue was never broadcast on the CBC.

I knew that sports stories always had great impact on the public. I discovered this in the mid-1970s when, in the middle of the Stanley Cup playoffs, back in the days when the Canadiens always were in them, I learned about a bizarre plot. Drug traffickers being watched by the RCMP wanted to kidnap star player Guy Lafleur and ransom him for a large sum of money. Police managed to foil the plot. But would a boxing story create a stir? I didn't know.

I dusted off the file in 1984, when I went back to working for a daily newspaper. I was hired by the *Journal de Montréal* somewhat by accident, and could have just as easily ended up with *Le Devoir* or returned to *La Presse*. My friend Claude Masson was *La Presse*'s news editor at the time. When I told him I was leaving television, he said there'd surely be reservations about my returning to the newsroom, particularly among journalists covering the crime beat. As for *Le Devoir*, I'd written for the paper on a few occasions, and the editor-in-chief at the time, Lise Bissonnette, was hoping to revive a beat that Jean-Pierre Charbonneau had successfully covered for her paper. Besides, *Le Devoir* had distinguished itself in this area in the 1950s, when Gérard Pelletier had written a long series of articles on corruption and commercialized vice in Montreal with Pacifique Plante, right-hand man to future mayor Jean Drapeau in a famous public clean-up campaign.

In my time with the CBC, I maintained good contacts with other crime reporters by regularly dropping in to the press room at the Montreal courthouse. That's where I told my friend Ives Beaudin that I planned to return to a newspaper. He mentioned this to his bosses, who immediately called me. The *Journal de Montréal* hired me in less than two hours, over lunch. The paper's management had decided to add another news-in-brief journalist to its weekend team since its competitor, *La Presse*, which published six days a week, had announced it would now appear Sundays.

As soon as I was hired, managing editor Jean-François Lebrun asked me whether I had any ideas. His jaw dropped when I told him I was working on the Hilton boxing family, which was under Frank Cotroni's control.

By the end of that year, there were three lawsuits filed against me with three Montreal dailies, besides another one targeting me jointly with the CBC. Though we were being asked to pay millions of dollars, all these suits were eventually dropped. Only one was settled out of court, the one brought against me by the Hiltons, who claimed I'd sullied their reputation. Tens of thousands of dollars were spent in legal fees before the file was closed. I asked that the Hiltons write me a cheque for one hundred dollars as compensation. I insisted on getting this cheque as a means of telling those suing me for various reasons that we'd defend ourselves to the end. However, I never found out if the cheque was cashed, or if the boxers' bank account had enough funds to cover it. As for their reputation, the Hiltons demolished it themselves. But in 1984, Davey Hilton was at the pinnacle of his glory. He might have reached the highest summits of boxing were it not for his lack of intelligence, or that of his family, and the Mafia's involvement.

On the Saturday in March after I began working at the *Journal de Montréal*, I prepared a series of articles announcing that the mandate of the Commission of Inquiry into Organized Crime (CIOC) was about to expire. I also described changes in the local mob over the last two years, explaining in detail the fall of the Cotroni empire and the rise of the Sicilian clan, lead by the Rizzutos, father and son. Nicolo and Vito Rizzuto had lived in exile but had returned to Montreal to regain lost ground. At the end of the article, a brief note said: "Tomorrow: boxing and the Mafia." The curiosity of my colleagues was piqued. Next day, the article titled "FRANK COTRONI GODFATHER TO HILTONS" would stir up the "wonderful world of sports" and the public in general. That Sunday, *La Presse* had expected to enjoy some media attention because of the launch of its new edition. Instead, my story about Mafia infiltration into boxing is what made headlines.

I'd obtained a copy of a police report written following an investigation called "Borgia" that dealt with Mafia ramifications in Montreal. For two years, officers from Montreal, the QPF, and the RCMP had been watching Frank Cotroni's gang. Detectives had discovered that Cotroni had spent large sums over the past four years to provide for the support, housing, transportation, and even training of the Hiltons. Cotroni's involvement with boxing provided a cover that allowed him to meet with criminal associates throughout the country. Besides controlling the young Hilton brothers, Cotroni also was a force to be reckoned with in the promotion of boxing. He took advantage of boxing galas to hold summit meetings. This was the case in Cornwall and Winnipeg, where I followed him for three days in June 1982. Cotroni had travelled under a false name, but he was given a king's welcome when he got off the plane. The police report also mentioned links between Cotroni and boxers Eddie Melo, Nick Furlano, and John Degazio. It also recalled that Melo had been arrested carrying a concealed weapon as he was leaving a nightclub with Frank Cotroni. The Mafioso then had to testify at the trial of the Toronto boxer, who was acquitted despite testimony from a police officer.

Montreal's Athletic Commission, a para-municipal organization that supervised combat sports at the time, admitted its powerlessness to investigate the Mafia. After my stories were published in 1984, the commission's president, Paul-Émile Sauvageau, asked Quebec Justice Minister Pierre-Marc Johnson to shed light on organized crime's infiltration of sports. Instead of launching a public inquiry, the justice minister mandated Quebec Court Judge Raymond Bernier to preside over a fact-finding committee that could call witnesses. A little more than a year later (in 1985), the judge tabled his report, after questioning 105 witnesses and confirming all the allegations made in the articles I'd written in March 1984. However, the government decided to keep the document secret. Judge Bernier only released the part of his report dealing with deficiencies noted in several regulations, as well as proposed solutions for improving the safety of sports and the lot of boxers. But the most interesting part, on the involvement of organized crime in professional sports, was kept secret. A real challenge for a journalist like me.

I started contacting people who I thought could help me get a copy of the famous secret report. It took months. Then, on April 12, 1986, I began publishing the complete findings pertaining to the Mafia's schemes. The Bernier Committee had confirmed that Cotroni was the heart and soul of boxing, that he'd invested a great deal of money in the careers of the "Fighting Hiltons," as they were called, and that his henchmen even tried to intimidate certain media bosses. The committee had discovered evidence proving that Cotroni imposed his views on promoter Henri Spitzer, who'd tried to downplay Cotroni's influence before the fact-finding committee. Judge Bernier had also concluded that Cotroni had sold the Hiltons to American promoter Don King. Finally, the committee had established that ten or so local Mafiosos and Toronto criminals controlled professional boxing.

Following this investigation, the career of the Hilton brothers, of Davey and Alex in particular, went from bad to worse. With the help of alcohol, the boxers began distinguishing themselves more on the street than in the ring. They were implicated in a holdup at a Dunkin' Donuts, the kind of establishment that criminals with the least intelligence avoid frequenting, because their clientele famously includes police officers. Fights and arrests increased. Then, on April 15, 1999, in what was likely the heaviest blow to his career, Davey Hilton was arrested and charged with sexually assaulting underage girls.

Before disclosing this story, I met Davey Hilton at the gym where he worked out in southwestern Montreal. Always polite, as is his habit when he isn't drunk, Hilton explained that the charges were nothing but a web of lies concocted by his wife, from whom he was separated. He said he was being framed and that he never assaulted the two teenagers. At the trial, however, Judge Rolande Matte didn't buy this story, choosing instead to believe the two young girls and ruling that Hilton was guilty. The prosecution asked for a seven-year sentence, while the defence argued that three years would be adequate. Given Hilton's lack of remorse, Judge Matte opted for the suggestion made by prosecutor Hélène Di Salvo, handing the boxer a seven-year sentence.

On October 15, 1985, at about 11 P.M., lawyer Frank Shoofey, the Hilton brothers' official manager, was gunned down at the door to his Cherrier Street office as he was returning from a hearing of Montreal's Athletic Commission. The commission had launched an inquiry into a boxing match that was to take place in Montreal a few days later. With my colleague, photographer Luc Bélisle, I'd spoken to Shoofey for several minutes at the doorway of the commission's office. Two hours later, he was shot several times in the head.

That crime remains unpunished, though the MUC police's homicide squad managed to identify the killers, go-betweens, and even the sponsors of the crime. A criminal admitted to the murder and denounced his accomplices, but the case was never tried. Police gave the talkative criminal a lie-detector test, but he lied about certain things, notably to protect an accomplice he didn't want to identify. How could police believe a witness who told the truth some of the time, and lied when it suited him?

Shoofey was known as a defender of widows and orphans, as well as of several major and minor criminals. His association with mobsters, however, frustrated his dreams of going into politics – the Liberal Party of Québec constantly rejected him as a candidate. Police remain convinced he was murdered because he defended the interests of the Hilton brothers too well. Shoofey had strongly opposed the contract with Don King. However, Cotroni made it happen by working through his own American lawyer. The day the contract was signed, Dave Hilton, Sr., had been given a lot to drink. He also pocketed a few tens of thousands of dollars and signed his sons' careers over to Don King. Though police have often tried to reopen the investigation into the lawyer's murder over the last fifteen years, it has always been in vain.

Another Cotroni protege met a similar fate in April 2001. Eddie Melo, having become a Cotroni henchman, was involved in all kinds of crimes in Toronto, and was gunned down leaving a sports bar in a Toronto suburb. Some people still dreamed of seeing Melo box in Montreal – he had been a star in his time.

During my career, which, all things considered, has been rather long, I never thought I'd met major or even minor international spies. However, long after I'd met certain respectable people, I discovered that they had other lives.

I met my first real spy inside the Saint-Vincent de Paul prison. Volunteers with the Arcade group had invited me to participate in a cultural activity with prisoners. An organizer of the event was former university professor Raymond Boyer, a distinguished man, a genuine aristocrat said to be immensely rich. Devoted to the cause of prisoners, he made it his duty to help the most destitute residents of the old Laval penitentiary. At the time, I didn't know that Boyer was also one of the few Canadians to have been condemned as a spy for the U.S.S.R.

The Soviet spy affair had started the Cold War with Moscow in the immediate aftermath of the Second World War. When he learned that he and his family were about to be sent home, a clerk with the Soviet embassy in Ottawa decided to defect and gave the game away. Igor Gouzenko took boxes of documents out of the embassy, but at first no one in the Canadian government wanted to deal with him. The diplomat-spy had to make two attempts before someone acted on his information. He later gave several interviews, trying to get better compensation in exchange for his collaboration. When he appeared on TV or gave interviews, he always wore a hood or a paper bag over his head. He died in 1982.

Boyer and eleven other people were arrested and sentenced for belonging to the vast Soviet spy network exposed by Gouzenko. The professor was given two years in prison for passing secrets to the U.S.S.R. through Fred Rose, the only member of the Canadian Communist Party to have been elected to the House of Commons. He was a doctor of chemistry when he'd passed over secrets concerning the RDX explosive, which was manufactured in a Shawinigan factory without any special surveillance. Moreover, Canada was ready to send samples of the explosive to Moscow at the end of the war, but the Allies had refused. Nonetheless, all documents on research done here were handed over to the Soviets. But it's for passing those documents through spy networks that the millionaire professor was sentenced. Boyer made a career change following his prison release, studying criminology to be in a better position to help former prison mates.

Gilles Brunet was the son of a former RCMP officer who became director of the Quebec Police Force, and who was called on to reform police behaviour following the death of Maurice Duplessis. In 1956, Josaphat Brunet, his father, had been appointed the first officer responsible for the RCMP's security and intelligence service in Montreal. He had a remarkable career.

Gilles Brunet was assigned to the RCMP's Section B in Montreal, the group in charge of watching foreign agents working for the U.S.S.R. and its satellites. He was highly respected. In the early 1970s, I had had a few discreet, if not secret, meetings with Brunet. At the time, I was interested in an important case concerning Soviet spying in Canada that involved the head of RCMP secret services in Ottawa, Leslie Jim Bennett. For months a rumour had been going around that Bennett was a spy. Of British origin, he was one of the first civilians to obtain a position in the police's high command. Brunet, just like many of his colleagues, was aware of the rumours and suspicions concerning the big boss.

Rumours aren't proof so there was no way I could write on the subject. In 1972, Bennett left the RCMP after being interrogated at length. Much later, in March 1993, he was cleared of all suspicions when a renegade Soviet spy disclosed the secret. Several years following Bennett's departure, Col. Oleg Kalouguine revealed that, for many years, the KGB had had a mole inside the RCMP's counterespionage service in Montreal. Only in 1991 was it uncovered that this mole was Gilles Brunet. Senior officers had launched an internal investigation. It was then confirmed that the lavish lifestyle the former police officer enjoyed was supported by the hundreds of thousands of dollars the Soviets said they paid him for his services. But is any of this true? Gilles Brunet died in 1984 from heart trouble. Eleven years before, the officer had had a long fight against his superiors, who were forbidding him from seeing Mitchell Bronfman, a member of the famous family of billionaires.

Brunet and Donald McCleary, his colleague and friend, knew Mitchell Bronfman socially. Moreover, the police had learned that the businessman also had ties with William Obront, financier to Vincent Cotroni, who headed the Canadian Mafia at the time. The two police officers refused to obey their bosses' orders and were finally dismissed. The RCMP's resolve in investigating Brunet was partially explained later by the revelation he was a traitor. But no one was ever able to shed light on this case, since Canadian authorities never disclosed any other information. The Brunet case died when he did.

Espionage stories have always fascinated the public, and the media delight in discovering and publishing amazing sagas or tantalizing affairs. One of these sensational stories was published on December 6, 1974, when *La Presse* revealed that a Soviet spy had been appointed by his country as a representative to the committee for organizing the 1976 Montreal Olympics. He was a kind of ambassador to the Organizing Committee for the Olympic Games (OCOG).

Over the years, I'd gathered good information on major and minor espionage affairs that had taken place nearly everywhere in the world. I'd indexed several public documents, newspaper articles, and books to easily find my way through the long list of characters who'd attracted attention. In 1974, I requested and obtained the personnel list of all countries represented on the OCOG. In fact, I was only interested in the identity of delegates from Eastern European, but had I asked only for this short list, my objective would have seemed too obvious.

Comparing this official list with my archives, I found a similar name in both: Aleksandr S. Gresko. To the British Secret Service, this man was a spy expelled from London in 1971 following the discovery of a huge spy network. To the Soviets, Gresko was vice-president of the sports ministry's international relations committee. Canadian hockey fans had heard about him, since he was a Moscow representative in the 1974 series between the Canadian and Soviet teams, the latter then being reputedly strong competition for the Canadian stars.

But even if the two names were identical, I still wasn't sure the sports representative and the spy were the same man. One of my good contacts, however, confirmed that the Gresko on the OCOG was the spy. When I asked whether a photo of this intriguing character was available, my counterpart guffawed, saying a photo of him with Prime Minister Pierre Elliott Trudeau had appeared in some papers. Gresko had participated in a sweater-swapping ceremony between the two teams in Trudeau's company. I found the photo in the newspaper archives. All I then had to do was contact the spy to ask for his comments.

The conversation didn't cost much in long-distance fees, however, because Gresko only answered a few questions. He said the charges against him were a web of lies fabricated by western intelligence services. He categorically denied that he'd done anything that was contrary to his status as a diplomat. He never returned to Montreal. My revelations were published, however. According to his colleagues, "His work was done."

In the days following this disclosure, Opposition parties had a field day in the Commons trying to embarrass the Trudeau government. An Opposition MP wondered whether Ottawa hadn't offended Great Britain by welcoming to Canada, and right into the Prime Minister's Office, a spy who'd been expelled from London three years earlier. The prime minister, however, was not overly perturbed. He said that the government and the RCMP knew what Gresko's activities had been before and during his trip.

The main reason given for the close surveillance of unions by secret services in the 1970s and 1980s was that they were being infiltrated by subversive elements. Keeping an eye on union members, however, required the use of informers. One of them was Marc-André Boivin, a Confederation of National Trade

Unions (CNTU) official in charge of organizing protests during labour conflicts. Boivin was a militant of the extreme left and an advocate of world peace. He was recruited as an informer by the RCMP's secret service, then transferred to the Canadian Security Intelligence Service (CSIS) when the organization was created to take over the role previously played by the federal police.

In June 1987, the QPF arrested four CNTU employees for placing bombs in a hotel belonging to businessman Raymond Malenfant. At the time, Malenfant was involved in a dispute with his employees at the famous Manoir Richelieu located in La Malbaie, in Quebec's Charlevoix region. What the police didn't know was that one of the detainees was a high-calibre CSIS informer. Learning about Marc-André Boivin's exact role, once again thanks to a good informer, I wrote an article on the subject, which *Le Journal de Montréal* published very prominently on page three. In this article, I related that this man had been working for the police and CSIS for years, and that he had even participated in special trips abroad and reported on them to his real bosses.

I published an excellent scoop that day. But even if my colleagues at the newspaper and I were proud of ourselves, it seems that no one in the CBC newsroom bothered to read our paper. Indeed, the following night, journalist Normand Lester reported the same news, claiming it was an exclusive!

This is the same Lester who, in September 1987, got a real scoop on Canadian intelligence. Lester was renowned for having many sources in that area. He did a major report mentioning that several Canadian unions had been infiltrated, including the Centrale de l'enseignement du Québec (CEQ), which has since become the Centrale des syndicats du Québec (CSQ). At the time, I thought that the CBC was only broadcasting a preliminary report, to be followed by other revelations in the coming days. Indeed, it's common practice in journalism to spread a series of major news items over several days to maintain the interest of readers or listeners.

After listening to Lester, I decided to publish a series of articles concerning an important character from Quebec's labour movement suspected of being a Moscow agent for the last twenty years at least. This kind of news can be read in foreign papers, but is rarely seen in Canada. I'd been gathering information on the Agnaïeff case for several years, awaiting the right moment to publish it. This was the time.

Michel Agnaïeff wasn't only a union official, he was also president of the New Democratic Party's (NDP) Quebec wing. He was executive director of the CEQ, the third most important labour federation in the province. Born in Egypt to Russian parents, Agnaïeff had immigrated to Canada in the 1960s. But shortly after his arrival, security services placed him under close surveillance, hardly ever losing sight of him for more than twenty years. The counterespionage service thought he was an agent of influence working for a foreign power.

When I interviewed him, he denied any foreign collusion, saying he was likely an ideal target for the police because he was born abroad of Russian parents and had worked for a Soviet company. Moreover, he said he'd participated in most of the major strikes and had belonged to Quebec's left-wing movement for the last twenty years. Agnaïeff had lodged a complaint against CSIS with the Security Intelligence Review Committee (SIRC), but the organization felt the authorities had good reasons for keeping him under such surveillance.

For nearly ten years, between 1963 and 1972, Quebec's terrorist movement was behind numerous events that would forever mark the history of our country. I was an inexperienced journalist when the Front de libération du Québec (FLQ) was created.

In 1964, I witnessed from a distance the arrest of a group of FLQ members who'd moved to the Mauricie to establish a training camp on a small farm in Saint-Boniface. The young journalist I was then obtained nothing important, all the news having been published by "old pros" from Montreal.

A few years later, during the major demonstrations of 1968 and the second wave of the FLQ, I knew how to obtain first-hand information. Accordingly, in 1970, when the October Crisis was triggered by the kidnapping of British diplomat James Cross, I was able to write an exclusive. The day following the abduction on Redpath Crescent, in downtown Montreal, I revealed that police were actively seeking Jacques Lanctôt. The link had been easy to establish. In March 1970, police officers patrolling on Saint-Denis Street had surprised two young men aboard a van containing a box big enough to hold a large adult. They had a sawed-off shotgun and a bundle of documents.

It was treated at first as a routine case, and went nearly unnoticed. The two men were charged with simple possession of a firearm. Police suspected the duo was getting ready to rob a store, but they were wrong. The two young men were going to kidnap the American consul in Montreal. It's only a few hours later, when detectives with the Montreal police's anti-terrorist squad saw the suspects' names on the list of people picked up in the last few hours, that the importance of the arrests were realized. Since that incident, Lanctôt had gone underground. After Cross's abduction in the fall, the methods used by the kidnappers and various evidence gathered by police left no doubt: Jacques Lanctôt was among the abductors.

In the two months that followed, exclusives streamed out of everywhere. One journalist who wrote several had had a long career with the *Toronto Star*, which is all to his credit. But I, a journalist with six years' experience in Montreal, guessed that it was in Montreal that my Toronto colleague obtained his best exclusives.

It was also obvious that his informers were RCMP officers. I then decided to also cultivate good contacts inside the RCMP.

At the time, the federal police had a rather simple communication policy. Journalists nearly always got the same answer: "No comment." I realized that federal agents were often successful in their fight against the drug business and that it was easier to loosen their tongues by asking about those achievements. The embarrassing questions regarding other topics would come later.

Following the October Crisis, I covered several espionage files and my determination to make new contacts would be well rewarded. Over the years, I also established a good network among the various police forces, mainly with the Montreal police – which later became the Montreal Urban Community Police Department – and the Quebec Police Force, whose name has changed at least four times during my career.

In 1975, I got a lot of satisfaction from writing a series of articles on police activities concerning the FLQ, particularly during the October Crisis. Through interviews with several of the inquiry's main players, I managed to relate in detail how police had been able to find James Cross and capture his abductors.

There have long been various and conflicting reports about the number and size of the FLQ's cells. Several individuals, including many journalists, wanted to create myths, often based on poorly interpreted facts or information that was either sketchy or false. Examples of twisted facts abounded during the 1970s. Many saw plots everywhere. Ottawa was thought to be responsible for various operations designed to counter the rise of Quebec's separatist movement. Many believed that foreign elements were at work in the province. Big business and the CIA were often thought to be working together.

One of the best examples of myth creation was the "Brinks stunt." It was during the provincial election campaign in April

1973 that a number of large companies based in Montreal supposedly organized the transfer of securities to Ontario to create panic among the population. This diabolical plan, it was believed in some circles, was intended to show that the election of Parti Québécois (PQ) members would cause a serious flight of capital out of the province. A Canadian Press photo printed on the *Montreal Star*'s front page showed uniformed personnel transferring large bags of securities from one armoured truck to another. What was actually happening was in fact very simple: an armoured truck had broken down and it contents were shifted to another one. Publication of this photo on election day in an English newspaper attracted no attention. People only started commenting on the incident the next day by misrepresenting it. Another myth was born.

The influence of foreign powers also prompted as many theories in the separatist camp as it did in the federalist one. However, in my experience, police intelligence officers have always taken great pains to sort the truth out from the lies in these theories about plots or infiltration in economic and especially political circles.

In October 1976, the world of Quebec politics was seething. The PQ was on a roll while everything was going badly for Robert Bourassa's Liberals, who were heading into an election campaign. The government had just been through several crises and a wind of scandal was blowing over Quebec. The number of "affairs" was increasing. Right in the middle of the election campaign, I revealed the existence of a top-secret service within the Quebec government: the Centre d'analyse et de documentation (CAD)*. The Bourassa government, wanting to diversify its

---

* The Centre for Analysis and Documentation.

intelligence gathering, had created the CAD to compile information from various sources, including police intelligence services. The CAD had exceptional means at its disposal and, at the time, laws protecting personal information weren't as restrictive as they are today. The service also kept an eye on several officials. Since no law controlled the use of bugs at the time, electronic surveillance was discreetly carried out by intelligence officers from major police forces.

The RCMP had no trouble eavesdropping since, according to various laws on national security and the Official Secrets Act, federal intelligence agents had free rein. Officially, the federal police didn't wiretap when dealing with criminal matters. Unofficially, the RCMP was secretly subsidizing the Westmount municipal police force, which was better equipped than all other police forces in Canada. One officer was assigned exclusively to manage the wiretapping service in a municipality where no investigation requires the use of such instruments. The Montreal and provincial police forces used this investigative technique to gather intelligence and frequently discovered crimes and caught criminals red-handed as a result.

One such case had to do with manipulation of the Montreal Forum's clock by Mafiosos from the Cotroni clan in the 1970s. The criminals had organized a lottery based on the minute and second when the last goal of a hockey game was scored. Fans knew – because statistics revealed – that the greatest number of goals are scored in the last minutes of a period. The lottery, although illegal, was very popular. An MUC police officer, Lieut. Steve Olynik, declared under oath during the trial of one clock manipulator that he'd personally observed that the clock operator would sometimes let the clock continue to run for a few seconds after a goal was scored. Turned out he was in the pay of the criminals.

In any event, because they had access to wiretap information, police officers and senior CAD officials had an incomparable store of information in their files, which it was said would allow them to better manage crises and better inform the government. The CAD was compared by critics to the FBI, the CIA, or even to the French DST. However, when confirming the centre's existence, Premier Robert Bourassa claimed it was a completely harmless service that only gathered information from public sources. He energetically denied it had committed any illegal actions.

The PQ, for its part, vehemently denounced this secret and special department. As soon as the election had been won, the new premier, René Lévesque, and his justice minister, Marc-André Bédard, announced that the CAD's archives would be destroyed and that the organization would be dismantled. The entire process was attended by a great deal of publicity. However, the government never confirmed that all CAD files had been destroyed. The centre had put together thirty thousand files on individuals and six thousand on organizations since its creation in 1971. Moreover, it was learned after the agency's dismantling that nearly two thousand files on specific events had been open. Its investigations into everything from the meetings of women's groups to student demonstrations were incredibly wide-ranging.

In the 1970s, constant tensions between Quebec City, Ottawa, and Paris held the attention of the public, the politicians, the police, and intelligence agents. Some people saw spies everywhere. One of those spies whose name was on everyone's lips was Philippe Rosillon. Prime Minister Pierre Elliott Trudeau had said Rosillon was a French spy assigned to help and fund Quebec separatist movements. Rosillon was close to certain terrorists and actively promoted the cause of French in Canada. He admitted he was behind the famous "Vive le Québec libre!" uttered by French president Charles de Gaulle during his renowned July 1967 speech from the balcony of Montreal's city hall. A dedicated supporter of Quebec independence and fervent promoter of the French fact in America, Rosillon was classified as undesirable by Canadian authorities and didn't set foot in Quebec again for five years. He was a member of the "Patrie and Progrès" network, a group of senior French officials dedicated to promoting French throughout the world. His actions were often unknown to his own bosses.

It was public knowledge that Ottawa was keeping a very close watch on several diplomats and officials with various French companies suspected of promoting Quebec independence. Ottawa's denunciations made headlines for two decades. However, what wasn't known at the time was that the QPF's intelligence service was also interested in Rosillon and other personalities linked to France as agents of influence and protectors of certain individuals, including at least one FLQ member who has since become a senior official in France.

For many years, the QPF had been conducting Operation Fleur-de-Lys, whose purpose was to demonstrate the influence of "subversive foreign agents Philippe Rosillon and Xavier Deniau" on various FLQ members. Thanks to a leak from the secret services, Conservative MP Tom Cossitt said in 1978 that Deniau was one of the spies France had working in Canada. Deniau has always been considered a great friend of the cause in Quebec City. He was secretary general of the International Association of French Speaking Parliamentarians and Premier René Lévesque awarded him the Order of Francophone Americans. Only several years following this investigation did I manage to get various documents, unpublished to this day, demonstrating the Quebec police's interest in French government agents and their influence over FLQ terrorists or Quebec government officials.

Gilles Stéphane Pruneau, who died a few years ago, was the only known FLQ member to avoid the wrath of the Canadian justice system. Pruneau was part of the FLQ's first wave. He was

nineteen years old in 1963, when he fled Canada to take refuge
first in France, then Algeria. The report of Operation Fleur-de-
Lys describes him as one of those responsible for the mailbox
bombings in Westmount. One of those explosions seriously
injured Walter Leja, an explosives expert with the Canadian
Armed Forces, who remained paralyzed for the rest of his life.
When the report was written, the fugitive was still accused of
having conspired in those bombings with FLQ members Mario
Bachand, Jean-Denis Lamoureux, François Gagnon, and Pierre
Schneider. Bachand was murdered in Paris on March 29, 1971,
in circumstances that remain mysterious. As for Lamoureux
and Schneider, they led quiet lives after serving prison sentences. Both became journalists and both were my bosses for a
few years.

Schneider was a crime reporter. Lamoureux, for his part,
was often vilified by a Quebec City radio host, who turned him
into his favourite scapegoat, particularly after he'd been
appointed press secretary to Premier René Lévesque. I never
had any problems with these two men, who did their work while
respecting the rules of our profession.

The Operation Fleur-de-Lys report said that Pruneau coor-
dinated the Quebec separatist movement's efforts from Algeria,
working as a liaison with the al-Fatah terrorist network that, in
1969, had provided $1,500 to the McGill Operation (a national-
ist demonstration against the university that was viewed as a
bastion of anglophone power). The author of the report, which
the QPF and provincial government had jealously kept secret,
tried to examine the role played by seven foreigners who had
been active in the FLQ. After infiltrating the separatist movement,
these characters, according to the report, had "tossed out the
idea that terrorism could be profitable. Their work inside this
movement allowed them to influence and indoctrinate militants

who were more likely to create the first Quebec cells and to structure a terrorist organization." The QPF officer who wrote the document wondered why these individuals had been prompted to act by authorities in certain foreign countries. He mentioned France and a Soviet bloc country, both of which acted through foreign nationals with ties to France.

The Operation Fleur-de-Lys report also mentioned the influence of "French agents," including Rosillon. The document contains a letter from Rosillon suggesting that the best way to help Quebec become a French and sovereign state would be to increase French immigration to the province. "The fate of Quebec," Rosillon wrote on November 24, 1967, "rests on the outcome of the immigration battle. All other aspects of the Quebec problem, including cooperation between France and Quebec, seem secondary, if not laughable, when compared to this issue."

Police established that Rosillon was linked to several senior Quebec officials, including some, of French extraction, who held strategically important positions within Quebec's immigration department. That QPF intelligence service had very good sources is shown by the lengthy excerpts from telexes sent abroad by senior Quebec officials that are transcribed in the report. The document also gave an extensive account of coded communications between several individuals that mentioned a "Centre," as well as former FLQ member Gilles Stéphane Pruneau's involvement in it.

The way the intercepted communications were written, and the use of a code, allowed police surveillance officers to conclude that activities were either clandestine or at the very least conducted for official purposes in a secretive way. Using information gathered through Operation Fleur-de-Lys, the QPF wanted to have two senior Quebec officials, one a deputy minister, the

other a major department head, classified as threats to state
security. The allegiance of these officials was to France rather
than to their employer.

To a journalist, there's no such thing as bad information, and
it's often very indirectly that we're put on the trail of a big story.
A case in point: one of my informers, at the end of the summer
in 1998, suggested I look into a commonplace arrest at the
Westmount municipal library for the theft of an ashtray.

This informer was reliable and I took the tip seriously. It was
the beginning of another wonderful journalistic adventure that
would yield good exclusives for my paper and me, as well as put
me on the trail of one of the largest international terrorist organizations, that of Osama bin Laden, the man the U.S. wants more
than anyone in the world.

This theft of an ashtray would also help me discover a part,
albeit tiny, of Canada's security intelligence world today. "The
more things change, the more they're the same," my informer
had told me, referring to the strange behaviour of CSIS
employees. He even claimed that the astonishing methods
used by RCMP intelligence services disclosed in the 1960s and
1970s were nothing compared to the tactics now used by CSIS
secret agents.

In the late 1970s, two commissions of inquiry, that of Judge
McDonald, created by Ottawa, and the Keable Commission,
created by Quebec City, examined the investigative methods of
intelligence officers against the FLQ, the separatist movement,
and other organizations both clandestine and official.

The ashtray lead wasn't easy to follow. The individual
arrested by an intelligence officer in June 1998 was a convert to
Islam, a dyed-in-the-wool Quebecer who'd become a passionate
defender of Islamic thought and given himself the mission of

propagating that doctrine in Canada. Let's call him Youssef, for the purpose of our story.

The RCMP's National Security Investigations Section was hot on the heels of Youssef. Federal agents suspected him of having threatened a French judge and having tried to provoke panic in the Montreal subway in March 1998 by saying he'd place a bacteriological bomb in it. He'd been under surveillance for several days when he went to the Westmount municipal library to use a public computer. Police didn't have an arrest warrant but had several facts linking him to the threats. One of the RCMP surveillance officers then saw the man slip an ashtray into his personal belongings. This was precisely the kind of incident that gave police officers the opportunity to intervene officially and legally. The RCMP informed a municipal security officer, who asked the visitor to empty his bag. The ashtray was found. Youssef was arrested and his belongings confiscated. Among his documents was a communique from the Islamic Jihad, in every way similar to eighteen other ones that had been sent to journalists and public officials. The document was submitted to expert analysis.

One of the communiques had been sent to the *Journal de Montréal*, warning that a bacteriological bomb had been placed in the Montreal subway. The authorities evacuated many of the stations, and a suspicious package was found at the Fabre station, on Jean-Talon Street. Though they aren't trained in handling bacteriological bombs, disposal experts with the MUC police's technical squad were dispatched to diffuse the device. If the device had turned out to be a bacteriological bomb, the police officers would have been very poorly protected. Fortunately, it turned out to be harmless.

Results of the writing analysis soon confirmed RCMP suspicions. Not only were most of the communiques produced by the same computer and printer, but DNA analysis and fingerprint comparisons linked the suspect to the envelopes used to send them. Youssef was never charged for stealing the ashtray, nor for the bomb threats, nor for sending the communiques. Nor was he charged for having sent letters to a French investigating magistrate, Judge Jean-Louis Brugière, who'd been assigned to get to the bottom of a series of bombings in France attributed to "Islamic terrorists," although he had undoubtedly sent these threatening letters too.

Youssef was well known by secret agents and police officers responsible for counterterrorism. What wasn't as well known, however, was that he was also a CSIS informer. So while civilian intelligence service bureaucrats were informing the government about the dangers of bio-terrorism at the dawn of the new millennium, an individual was using federal money to send threats signed Abu Jihad to newspapers and other organizations.

This disclosure would provoke a virtual war between the RCMP and CSIS. Since CSIS officials weren't responding quickly enough or were hiding too many things from their RCMP counterparts, the latter even requested a warrant to search the federal security service's files!

The threats against Judge Brugière were no minor matter, given the Parisian magistrate's importance. A specialist in investigating Islamic terrorist business in France, the judge established a solid reputation by going after the nabobs of international terrorism. He had dealt with Illich Ramirez Sanchez, alias Carlos, the world's number-one terrorist for a quarter-century. Carlos had committed numerous deadly attacks, including the infamous and brazen assault on Munich's Olympic village in 1972, which had cost the lives of several Israeli athletes. He was finally sentenced and imprisoned in France.

Since 1996, Judge Brugière had been on the trail of another Islamic network, whose operations centre was in Montreal.

According to French investigations, the group leader was Fateh Kamel, an Algerian who'd obtained Canadian citizenship. This importer had married a Quebec woman and lived with her and their children on Île Perrot, in Montreal's west end. He led an apparently quiet life.

Though Kamel vigorously denied being involved with international terrorism, a French newspaper described him in 2000 as the Carlos of Islamic terrorists. International investigations linked him to a network of extremists who had been trained in the Afghan war and who were now funded by the master of terror, Saudi millionaire Osama bin Laden. Police officers in the West think bin Laden was behind the Montreal group.

Judge Brugière had travelled to Montreal several times since 1996 to investigate Kamel. The powers of a French investigating magistrate are very broad. He can order that a suspect be remanded in custody for a long time. While in Canada, it seems the judge was rather frustrated at not being able to act as effectively as he could in France. Since the two legal systems are very different, a warrant for Kamel's arrest couldn't be obtained in Montreal. However, his arrest was only delayed, since the travelling Montrealer was stopped and questioned in Jordan and deported to France. In Paris, he was accused of helping terrorists. His name was associated with radical or terrorist groups in Italy, Turkey, France, and Canada. Some called him Mustapha the terrorist; others, El Fateh or simply Fateh.

French and Canadian authorities were seeking proof that people living in Canada were involved in an operation designed to provide Islamic terrorists with equipment that would allow them to detonate a nuclear bomb. Osama bin Laden allegedly had offered confrères US$1.5 million to buy uranium and other components to build an atomic device to intensify his holy war against the United States.

Judge Brugière had undertaken to follow Fateh Kamel's trail based on information obtained in Roubaix, near Lille, France, during the demolition of a building where a group of terrorists had taken refuge. Instead of surrendering, the besieged individuals had set fire to their apartment and shot at police officers. Four terrorists died. To fund its activities, this group had committed major armed robberies.

Kamel was the link between passport forgers and someone able to obtain real ones from the Canadian government under false pretenses. The trail of the French judges having led them to Montreal, the RCMP discovered the secret in an Anjou apartment where compromising documents were found. The list of phone calls made from this modest apartment on place de la Malicorne revealed that members of an international network were involved at various levels in preparing shocking operations or in assisting terrorists. Many of the individuals contacted by tenants of the apartment were associated with religious or humanitarian organizations that cloaked terrorist units.

The Anjou apartment had lodged several individuals over the previous months, including, mainly, Ahmed Ressam, Mustapha Labsi, and Abdel Boumesbeur, three Algerians who obtained political refugee status in Canada, and one Bosnian called Saïd Atmani, whom many people knew by the nickname of Karim. It was the headquarters of the Montreal mujahedeen cell whose boss was Karim.

Atmani was considered to be Fateh Kamel's right-hand man. Ressam ran a small business, as did Kamel, while other members got money from minor frauds and thefts committed in cars parked in downtown Montreal. During a memorable press conference on December 16, 1999, MUC police revealed that these men lived in poverty and used part of their earnings to "help the cause." Only once in a blue moon do journalists get to attend a press conference where police speak openly about investigations that usually take place amid the greatest secrecy. The police were claiming that the network of thieves was in league with Islamic terrorists.

That same morning, I learned that a certain Ahmed Ressam, who lived in Montreal, had been arrested the previous day trying to enter the United States with four powerful bombs. This was a few days from the new millennium and the news would attract a great deal of attention. Ressam, who had been the subject of investigations in Montreal, had dropped out of sight completely. It would later be learned that he had travelled to Afghanistan to train for higher functions within the organization. Afghanistan is where most Islamic terrorists got their training. Many of them had gone there in the 1980s to fight the Soviet invader alongside their Muslim brothers. Afterwards, many of them were used by Osama bin Laden, who set up al-Qaeda, in a secret corner of the country. From there, he has spread his war against the enemies of Islam around the world in ways we now know too well.

It was surprising to see Ahmed Ressam, who was travelling from British Columbia, reappear in Port Angeles, Washington. A routine check is all it took to prompt his arrest. Border officials noticed that the newcomer was nervous, identifying himself with a Costco card instead of a driver's licence. Pressed by increasingly pointed questions from the immigration officer, Ressam tried to run. Several agents caught him a few blocks away. He identified himself with fake documents, using the name Beni Alexandre Noris and Mario Roig, and claimed he lived in an apartment on du Fort Street in Montreal. He said he was twenty-eight years old. A piece of paper was found in his pocket bearing the name Ghani and the phone number of a Brooklyn apartment. Fingerprint analysis helped officers

confirm that the name of the captured terrorist was Ressam.
This arrest quickly caught the attention of investigative agencies
throughout the United States.

I wrote about the Montreal terrorist's arrest in the *Journal de
Montréal* on December 17, 1999. What I didn't know at the time
was that very few details concerning the arrest had filtered out,
because of the extreme nervousness of American authorities following the completely accidental discovery of a major terrorist
plot. I was very surprised that the publication of information I
discovered in Montreal would lead to one of the major scoops of
my career.

Immediately following the terrorist's arrest, American
authorities launched Operation Borderbom amid the greatest
secrecy. It was headed by the FBI and an anti-terrorist team set
up in the U.S. following the 1998 bombings of American
embassies in Kenya and Tanzania, which had killed 280 people,
including nine Americans. Details concerning the arrest of
Ressam, who had now been positively identified, were released
only a few hours after the publication of our paper, along with
news of his Seattle court appearance. The FBI also bugged the
phone of the man called Ghani, who was in fact Abdel Ghani
Meskini. Once arrested, he confessed his crimes and said he was
ready to testify.

A few days later, I obtained the only existing photo of
Ressam, taken after his arrest for fraud a few years earlier. To
this day, it remains the only photograph of the character to have
been published by the media, except for the bleary one where an
individual is seen in the back seat of a police car being taken to
the courthouse following his arrest.

And a few days later still, when Moktar Haouari, another
suspect in this affair, was arrested, I obtained a photograph
whose publication would cause quite a misunderstanding. A
CSIS agent, I was later told, had wrongly identified Haouari

during a surveillance session in a public place. The photograph I had published was the wrong one, so the newspaper and I had to make amends. Informing readers about such a mistake is one of the worst things a journalist or newspaper has to do. In this case, I did an interview with the individual wrongly identified as the one arrested by police, and we placed the new article in a very prominent place. We also published a detailed clarification to explain once and for all the circumstances leading to this mistake.

The investigation led to several developments. I was the one who had discovered the secret residence at place de la Malicorne. Thanks to several documents obtained from official sources, and various investigations by Canadian, American, and European journalists, the importance of the Montreal terrorist group was becoming more obvious.

At a press conference on April 6, 2000, the U.S. government offered a $5-million reward for the capture of Abdelmajid Dahoumane, Ressam's friend and associate from Montreal. Dahoumane, also of Algerian extraction, was suspected of being Ressam's accomplice in the American terrorist plot. He apparently had assembled the bombs with Ressam in a Vancouver motel. Never had so much money been put forward in Canada for a police investigation. It was, however, the second time that Washington was offering so much money for the capture of a terrorist, the first having been for Osama bin Laden, himself. Dahoumane was arrested in Algeria in 2000. Since then, the American state department and the CIA have been trying to convince Algerian authorities to hand Dahoumane over to U.S. justice officials.

Ahmed Ressam remained impassive in the dock when jurors returned from their deliberations on April 7, 2001, to render a verdict of guilty. He was accused of terrorism and importing explosives to the United States. The jury deliberated for ten hours to reach this conclusion. The same day, a Paris court sentenced him in absentia to five years in prison for helping terrorists, as it did for Abdel Boumesbeur and Abdellah Ouzghar, two other Montrealers linked to the same cell.

Fateh Kamel, for his part, got eight years in prison and banishment from French territory following his sentence. The prosecutor, Marc Trévédic, had been particularly incisive about Kamel's role within the cell. "Fateh Kamel is an important member of the Armed Islamic Group, which is linked to the international Jihad, having sought false documents to commit terrorist actions targeting France."

Moktar Haouari, after contesting his extradition to the United States for months, finally relented. He also is accused of terrorism. Mustapha Labsi, arrested in Great Britain, will eventually be tried in Paris.

9

The Bikers in My Life

Throughout my career, I've devoted a lot of time and effort to searching through files on major criminals linked to the Mafia in Canada and elsewhere. However, when I began writing on small biker gangs active in the late 1960s, I never thought these two-bit criminals would become so powerful. My interest in bikers emerged gradually and never did I imagine this type of specialized work would upset my career and life.

The first time I saw a Hells Angel was when visitors from around the world flocked to Montreal for Expo 67. The exposition was Mayor Jean Drapeau's pet project and effectively put Montreal on the world map. Hells Angels from Boston also got the idea of travelling to Montreal. The police were used to dealing with Saint-Laurent Boulevard heavies, so the bikers didn't scare them. Two officers prompted by curiosity stopped a group of bikers and asked that they come to the station on Ontario Street to answer a few questions. Police officers and bikers seemed to be having a good time when I dropped by to see what was going on. The incident had no follow-up.

Back then, young toughs from every corner of the province began wanting to imitate American bikers, whose exploits were reported by the media and glorified by Hollywood. At first, many of our would-be bikers were too young or didn't have enough money to buy motorcycles, but things would soon change.

In Montreal, the Popeyes were very active in the Lafontaine Park sector, while the Devils Disciples were starting to give the police problems in Villeray and Rosemont. Both groups consisted mainly of francophones. However, anglophones in the west end of the city wouldn't allow themselves to be outdone. The Satan's Choice seemed more powerful and prosperous than their friends in the east end. Established in the Saint-Henri neighbourhood, made famous by the Dubois brothers for a generation, the Choice, as they were called in the area, had already developed interests in the drug trade, dealing mainly in chemicals. The gang had its own amateur chemists who learned quickly from the experts. They also imported products and recipes from the United States.

This drug production was soon copied by the Disciples and the Popeyes, who quickly became masters at mixing chemicals. Marijuana was also fashionable, and bikers began to take an interest in that too. Bikers had previously been petty criminals who robbed houses and businesses and stole cars. Police essentially rebuked them for making noise, disturbing the peace in bars, and attacking young people who didn't like bikers pushing them around.

Gradually, those wearing the Popeyes' crest began to worry citizens, but the police still considered them to be minor hoodlums. Some groups in the province had taken to attacking young women and gang rapes tarnished the image of those associated with the gangs. The Popeyes had several circles or budding "chapters" in Trois-Rivières, Sorel, Drummondville, Hull, and Montreal. None of these clubs really had exclusive operating territories until the mid-1970s, when gangs became better organized. By then, bikers were starting to have more money and were increasingly feared.

The Devils Disciples didn't last long because the gang was split by a rivalry between two of its main bosses. Its leaders were eliminated one by one, as were many subordinates. Those who survived the slaughter pursued careers either on their own or in small groups, particularly in the drug trade. A quarter-century later, a few old members still had their crests and would occasionally go riding together. However, they avoided shouting from rooftops that the gang was still active. Police had forgotten about them as a group, even though some of the gang's most notorious members were still being watched individually.

The Satan's Choice were first to join one of the two large American gangs – the Outlaws – while the Popeyes made overtures to the Hells Angels. This change in our small gangs had an immediate impact on the tranquility of Montreal streets. To establish themselves in their new territory, the Hells Angels wanted to intimidate the Outlaws, who responded in kind. Pistol shots are what bikers used to hail each other. In the days of the Popeyes, war had already broken out with the Devils Disciples, who got along rather well with the Satan's Choice. From 1978 onwards, police noted that some murders committed in Montreal were due simply to rivalry between the two groups.

I discreetly visited the gangs' neighbourhoods several times. The Hells Angels had chosen a small house on Saint-Vallier Street, near Saint-Zotique Street, with a rather large garage at the back. The building had been fortified, and the bikers had put in new windows to keep better watch over the lane and spot the arrival of enemies or the police. Police visited rather frequently. Bikers sometimes slept outside, near the lane, when the temperature was too hot. The sound of bikes backfiring in the lane was an irritant to neighbours, who didn't dare voice their disapproval too loudly. Very soon, however, the bikers understood that the police wouldn't let them set up in the area peacefully. Successive raids forced the Hells Angels to find new gathering places. That's how the group moved to the Frenière concession road, near Saint-Eustache, as well as to Prince Street in Sorel.

Everywhere in Quebec, bikers got bad press: they were constantly being charged for rowdiness and fighting. They would storm into certain establishments and get drinks under threat. Some small towns experienced entire weekends of terror when biker hordes passed through. The Hells Angels were the worst of the kind. The Outlaws also had similar problems with police.

In 1979, I wrote a long series of articles for *La Presse* comparing bikers with the Mafia, concluding that bikers were the more powerful. In fact, they were far more murderous than Mafiosos, whose activities were becoming more discreet. But the power of bikers was far from its peak, which would be achieved in the 1990s.

This is when the Hells Angels increased their use of dynamite to secure their supremacy over other groups. In 1976, two Popeye members were killed while on their way to place a bomb in the subway to show support for imprisoned colleagues who were denouncing their living conditions. The man later chosen as national president of the Canadian Hells Angels, Robert "Tiny" Richard, also had an unfortunate experience: a bomb blew up in his face while he was making it, costing him an eye and leaving him partially handicapped.

Near the end of the 1970s, the Commission of Inquiry into Organized Crime (CIOC) made a timid foray into the world of bikers. The commission, which had had major success in dealing with the Dubois brothers and the Cotroni clan, came up short where bikers were concerned. Admittedly, it had some success in parts of the province when local biker leaders and their minions were summoned to their deliberations. Whether in Montmagny or Chicoutimi, police greeted the CIOC with open arms. However, save for a few arrests and spectacular hearings, the commission didn't put an end to gang activities. Commissioners didn't take on bikers in Montreal, where the three largest gangs operated, nor in Sherbrooke, where bikers were known as the Gitans.

Members of the Hells Angels put order and organization into their own group. They welcomed the wealthy Sherbrooke bikers into their ranks, and reorganized the provincial control structure. Many bikers who had distinguished themselves in their regions became members in good standing of the Hells Angels or affiliated clubs. Though the number of clubs decreased dramatically, bikers weren't deserting drug distribution territories. They were beginning to set up a hashish and cocaine network that would secure their power and wealth for the next twenty years at least.

At about the same time, the Angels got rid of their enemies. In 1979, a group of former Devils Disciples, who'd formed the Huns gang in Laval, lost their president, who was shot down by the Angels' two most prolific killers. I obtained a photograph of the Angels' number-one killer, Denis "Curé" Kennedy, posing in a field with four revolvers in his belt and two submachine guns in his hands, behind an older model machine gun mounted on a tripod. After publication of this rather spectacular photo, Kennedy gave an interview to a weekly paper, denying he was a killer working for the gang.

The Curé and some of his friends decided to found a new Angels club, the North chapter, while the others moved to Sorel but continued to call themselves the Montreal Hells Angels. The North chapter, which set up in a large garage on Arthur-Sauvé Boulevard, became known for extravagance. Bikers were always partying, and consuming cocaine had become the leading leisure pastime of some members. In 1982, Denis Kennedy and Charles Hachey were victims of a purge. Their corpses had been tied up inside sleeping bags weighed down with chains and cement blocks and thrown from the Lavaltrie wharf into the St. Lawrence River. "They consumed more coke than they sold," a gang member later said. Not liking their colleagues' methods, some left the Laval group to join their friends in Sorel. This split apparently happened without excessive violence. Or, if friction did occur, nothing leaked out.

The North chapter also became notorious for murders and drug trafficking on a very large scale. The gang was associated with Peter Frank Ryan, called Doony, boss of the West End Gang, which was involved in international drug trafficking on a scale rarely seen for an independent group in Canada. The North chapter ran Ryan's errands, going so far as to collect debts from other members of Canadian Hells Angels chapters. This was too much for the bikers, who were starting to be fed up with the Laval guys, who'd become uncontrollable. That's why a diabolical plot was hatched to eliminate the entire Laval group in one fell swoop. Since retiring them was out of the question, a wholesale purge was planned. All North chapter members who were to be present at a meeting in Lennoxville, allegedly to discuss the ambitions of an enemy gang, the Outlaws, were to be executed.

The date chosen for the great slaughter was Saturday, March 23, 1985. Ten or so members and close associates were on the list of people to be killed. The other members would have to join the Sorel gang or leave the organization. But the North chapter bikers – especially some of the older members – were suspicious. They decided to ignore the call made by the Sorel people, who'd summoned all Quebec members, as well as those from Halifax, to the Lennoxville bunker. Since only three North chapter members came to the fateful meeting, the bosses postponed the party to the next day, insisting the North chapter delegates convince their colleagues to show up.

The day of the crime, five bikers were killed, wrapped up and thrown into the St. Lawrence River from the wharf mooring the ferry that crosses from Saint-Ignace-de-Loyola to Sorel. Gilles Lachance, nicknamed Le Nez, was spared because of his exemplary behaviour. However, he later became an informer and contributed to the sentencing of many of those responsible for planning the murders.

A few days following the carnage, police learned of the sudden disappearance of Laurent Viau, nicknamed l'Anglais, the chapter's big boss; of Jean-Guy Geoffrion, called Brutus, the group's specialized mechanic; and of Jean-Pierre Mathieu, called Matt le Crosseur. Also missing were Michel Mayrand, nicknamed Willie, the drug trafficking supervisor for numerous south shore establishments, as well as Guy-Louis Adam, nicknamed Chop, a member who took up a lot of space. Another missing person was later added to the list: Claude Roy, nicknamed Coco, who'd been spared at first since he was one of the few North chapter bikers to know where the group stashed its drugs and money. The murderers were hoping to get their hands on the loot.

This wasn't the first time Hells Angels killed some of their members, but the extent of the Lennoxville massacre was unparalleled in the bikers' history. Régis "Lucky" Asselin and Yves "Apache" Trudeau were among the skeptics who'd refused to attend the meeting and managed to survive, the first having always had incredible luck, the other deciding to go into detox at Oka.

The contract to murder Asselin was offered to Trudeau, who, in exchange, could get his motorcycle back, which the Hells Angels had confiscated, as well as the $45,000 the murderers had found in the North chapter's safe in Laval. Asselin was finally killed a few years later by an aspiring biker who, on the same day, obtained his "colours," the official emblem, as well as his Hells Angels membership card. Louis "Melou" Roy rapidly became a star of the Canadian Hells Angels. Despite his status, he was also done in, on June 22, 2000, two days before the anniversary of the Trois-Rivières club's creation, of which he was founding president. His colleagues in the Nomads section felt Melou wasn't being honest in lowering the price of his cocaine kilos. His personal effects and assets were shared among "brothers" shortly after his official disappearance.

Trudeau had more luck. Three killers were sent to the Oka detox centre to execute him, but too many witnesses were present for them to carry out the job. Trudeau was arrested a few days later and sentenced to a year in jail in April 1985 for carrying an illegal weapon. Two months later, while serving his sentence at Bordeaux, the Montreal detention centre, he contacted the Quebec Police Force to inquire what the consequences would be should he choose to confess.

This was the first time a biker of Trudeau's status offered to become an informer, and Cpl. Marcel Lacoste of the QPF's predatory crimes squad could hardly believe his ears. For weeks, Lacoste had been trying to get Trudeau to collaborate. Police knew Trudeau was one of the most prolific killers Canada had known. His name had been linked to some fifty murders in Quebec over the last fifteen-odd years. He later admitted to having committed forty-three involuntary homicides and was condemned to life in prison. However, he was quickly subjected to a peculiar detention regime and regained his freedom in short order. Some felt Trudeau got off lightly considering his crimes;

however, the Crown couldn't have condemned him had he not admitted his guilt. Police had never been able to gather enough evidence to bring him before the court. The killer's statement was made against the promise his confession could never be used against him.

Trudeau himself didn't know how many murders he had committed. Though he was ready to admit everything, the police had to call on me and another specialized journalist to pull out some of our files concerning crimes he *might* have committed. Even with our assistance, Trudeau was not sure which murders could be added to his gruesome list. He admitted to killing one of his former colleagues, Jean-Marc Deniger, nick-named Boston, the Popeyes' former secretary, while he was the group's president. The reason: he absolutely wanted to get his shiny Harley-Davidson back, even by colluding with those who wanted to kill him. The Hells Angels wholeheartedly wanted to eliminate Deniger, who swore in every possible way that he wanted to avenge a friend killed during the purge. Trudeau killed Deniger by strangling him. The body was abandoned on a city street, but no one alerted police to its presence. Trudeau phoned the *Journal de Montréal* himself to tell journalists a corpse covered with a sleeping bag was in a car parked on de Normandville Street.

Naturally, I was the journalist who disclosed that Trudeau had collaborated with police and the law.

My coverage of the Hells Angels and the Lennoxville slaughter yielded several exclusives. Over many months, I published the equivalent of several books on the developments of this major police investigation. Together, these articles could probably make up an encyclopedia on the twisted world of bikers. During two coroner's inquests in Joliette and various legal proceedings,

I was in regular contact with the large Hells Angels family. Bikers had dubbed me "Auger les Abeilles" (Auger the bee man) because of my experience as a beekeeper. Some of them even told me bluntly I should return to being a farmer. I regularly observed their dissatisfaction with my many descriptions of their way of living, earning money, and, especially, of dying.

In those days, members of the Hells Angels were more willing to talk to journalists than they have been recently. As soon as the investigation of the Lennoxville slaughter began, six Sherbrooke bikers visited their biker friends in Paris. They claimed they weren't hiding, that they had travelled to France for pleasure. I reached the Angels' Paris chapter by phone. Someone named Loulou agreed to answer a few questions, though he wasn't very talkative. I didn't have much luck either with another French biker called Joël. Finally, by insisting, I managed to speak to Georges Beaulieu, called Bo-Boy, who was president of the Sherbrooke chapter. He was later condemned for his role in the massacre, having purchased the sleeping bags used to bury the corpses.

Bo-Boy claimed point-blank that the police had gone fishing. "The story about the corpses is unfounded," he said. "It's fine to say there are corpses, but where the fuck are they?" He also claimed that, contrary to police allegations, nothing had happened inside his club. Though he said he didn't want to be interviewed, he still spoke to me for more than fifteen minutes. He said he wasn't crazy about newspapers. "We have enough problems with the police on our backs without having to get the media involved," he added. He preferred to let the lawyers talk. "They know what should or shouldn't be said."

A few months later, when revelations about biker crimes were on the increase, another gang member agreed to give me an interview. Bob was and still is a member in good standing of the Hells Angels. He said he wanted to give the bikers' side of the story, since the police version of the Lennoxville slaughter is the one the media reported daily. At the time, Bob looked like a student; today, he could easily pass for a college teacher. Back then, he was trying to improve the image of his club and his friends. "The Hells Angels are here to stay, and police won't get rid of the club," he said. He felt that the police were deliberately trying to give bikers a bad image and reputation. "For us," he said, "the days of greasy, oily guys who terrorize people is over." Bob claimed without smirking that the Angels were simply an incorporated commercial business. Sensing my skepticism, he added, still seriously, that the bikers earned money from selling parts and motorcycles.

A founder of the first Quebec group to join the Hells Angels on December 5, 1977, Bob is among the rare ones to have survived. Some of his colleagues were murdered, others died in accidents or from natural causes. Later, I ran into Bob while heading to an evening performance at Place-des-Arts. Accompanied by his spouse, he spoke to me as though I were an acquaintance. I introduced him to my wife and to the couple accompanying us. Following this polite exchange, we went our separate ways. My brother-in-law didn't believe me when I told him a few moments later that he'd just shaken hands with the secretary treasurer of the Hells Angels, Inc.

The format and writing style of the *Journal de Montréal* were perfectly suited to our coverage of circumstances surrounding the death of the bikers. Tabloids require several photos to go along with articles. Photos of the bikers, their nicknames, various expressions and customs allowed us to write countless pages, most of them rather different, from day to day.

Some bikers didn't like the articles, while others were annoyed at the photographs. One day, a Sherbrooke chapter Hells Angel, Claude Berger, hailed me concerning the headline given to one of my articles. The previous day, I'd written that this biker was a music teacher at the Sherbrooke Cégep and third trumpet with the Quebec City Symphony Orchestra. He was really upset at having been the subject of an article and he'd especially disliked the title: "SOUR NOTE AT THE QUEBEC SYMPHONY: A HELLS ANGEL." I had to explain that a journalist can suggest titles for his articles, but, in the end, the news desk officer lays them out and has the last word.

I've often used the example of that title to show how layout is an important element that completes the journalist's research and writing. Photographers are also important. A newspaper's strength surely resides in the sum of the qualities of all its artisans. Where titles are concerned, humour is a useful tool, even if subjects don't appreciate it.

Police had a lot of success in their probe of the Lennoxville slaughter, since the QPF was already investigating bikers whose activities affected every region of the province. The QPF had set up Operation Haro to counter the gangs. In the days immediately following the bloodbath, detectives discovered the evidence they needed: the Hells Angels were down for the count. Most key players got sentences of several years to life in prison. Police congratulated themselves on their success. Many believed that the Hells Angels had been demolished and annihilated. They were way off the mark, since the gang quickly reorganized, heeding all the lessons learned from the Lennoxville affair. A new generation of Hells Angels soon showed their face.

Rising stars in the gang came from several Quebec regions, as well as Montreal. A few newcomers were from the SS club, friends of the Angels located in Pointe-aux-Trembles, in Montreal's east end. One of the group's leaders was Maurice "Mom" Boucher, called la Vieille (Old Lady) at the time by his friends. Another was Normand Hamel, dubbed Biff. These characters had many friends in their group, including brothers Salvatore and Giovanni Cazetta, who later founded the Rock

Machine. The two brothers decided not to join the Angels at the time because they wanted to remain independent and carry on with their various businesses. This is why their group was never a motorcycle gang, though their operations are exactly the same. Only the initials MC, for motorcycle club, were missing for the Rock Machine to be an official gang.

I'm the one who disclosed the existence of this gang that wasn't one on July 25, 1992. The group of eleven founding friends had chosen to set up in an old location already occupied by another biker gang in Montreal's east end, near the Jacques-Cartier Bridge. In 1993, when frictions started to emerge among drug traffickers, two Rock Machine leaders agreed to meet me in their bunker. Renaud Jomphe and Gilles Lambert wanted to explain that they and their friends weren't interested in becoming a biker club, that they weren't in the process of appropriating territory. "There's no biker war," they said. The fight began only a year later, despite declarations of peace from the Rock Machine. Their enemies had taken the lead.

In August 1995, Jomphe, who became president of the group, gave me an interview two days after the explosion that killed an innocent child, Daniel Desrochers. Jomphe insisted that I accurately report his comments. He said at the outset of our conversation that he wouldn't use the name of a rival biker gang, and didn't utter the words "Hells Angels" during the hour we talked about the Quebec crime scene. Jomphe had a message to send: "We're not the ones who kill children." He insisted his group hadn't started anything.

From the outset of the war, in 1994, it was obvious that former friends had become bitter enemies. A long list of murders would follow. This war ultimately claimed nearly 160 victims, including twenty or so people who had absolutely nothing to do with biker activities. They felt invincible, able to eliminate the competition, and thought they could stand up to political, legal, and police authorities. They intimidated police officers and took on prison guards and journalists. Robert Savard, a loan shark close to Maurice Boucher, even published a newspaper designed to denounce police, with former police officer Gaétan Rivest, who'd also become a loan shark, among other things. Savard tried to intimidate me with this newspaper, or pamphlet rather, by publishing a photograph of my home. What he didn't know, however, was that I no longer lived there at the time of publication. Savard tried to scare me several times. This sturdy fellow, whom I often met in my travels around the city, really didn't like either my reporting style or my constant targeting of his friends and colleagues. He was killed in April 2000 with several shots to the head while having breakfast in Montreal North. Though far from being among those I'm inclined to mourn, I feel Savard was somehow lucky to go this way. He surely didn't know he was going to die, since the killers acted so rapidly. All the same, I spared a thought for his close relatives, for his wife and child, who lost someone important.

Since 1995, public opinion in Quebec and Canada has become increasingly concerned about bikers and criminals in general. When eleven-year-old Daniel Desrochers was killed by shrapnel from a Hells Angels bomb, police forces combined their efforts. They put an end to their petty turf wars, joining forces and creating a specialized squad named Wolverine, after the animal that can become extremely aggressive when attacked. They made hundreds of arrests, dismantled several networks, picked up numerous informers, but were never able to charge those responsible for setting the bomb that killed the Desrochers boy.

The Hells Angels had placed a bomb in a Jeep to kill an enemy involved in a plot to murder Maurice Boucher, a leading character in the biker war, who was starting to be called the

Angels' warlord. However, the aggressors didn't know that the Jeep they had booby-trapped didn't belong to Normand "Bull" Tremblay, but rather to Marc Dubé, one of his friends, also a drug trafficker. The day before the explosion, Dubé had purchased from Tremblay his fancy "mag" wheels and installed them on his Jeep. This seemingly innocuous exchange of wheels led to a fatal confusion.

The bombers were located near the scene of the crime. They activated the device by calling the pager connected to the dynamite. An informer later explained to police that the bomb had been made in his garage, in the Rosemont neighbourhood. He related how a pensioner, his son, and other individuals had assembled the bomb in front of him. Three Hells Angels, he said, were linked to the bombing. Only one is still alive. He was never arrested.

As for the two other murderers, their own associates did them in. The corpses of Donald Magnussen and his boss, Scott Steinert, were found inside sleeping bags weighed down with chains and cement blocks along the banks of the St. Lawrence River. Both had been beaten to death. The Hells Angels eliminated their brothers, not because of Daniel Desrocher's death, but because the pair had been mixed up in the murder of a criminal whom the Angels had invited to Halifax. Magnussen had settled an old account with the visitor and Steinert hadn't prevented him.

Since the informer stopped collaborating with police, the case concerning the Desrochers boy's killers was never brought before a judge. On March 27, 1997, following publication of articles linking the Hells Angels to Desrochers's death, the Angels' Nomads chapter decided to put out a press release. This was the first time in my career as a journalist that I saw the gang issue a release explaining its position. The Angels denied their members had anything to do with the explosion that killed the

Desrochers boy, while denouncing what they considered to be a police disinformation campaign. The bikers were unabashedly saying they deplored the media's complacency "in this sinister smear campaign against our group." The release demonstrated the bikers' arrogance and self-assurance before the law. The author of the anonymous document, written on the group's official letterhead, invited police to charge the suspected member. "He'll then get a real trial, instead of a media lynching." The release's conclusion is the most astonishing part: "His innocence will be legally established."

The Desrochers boy's death changed my way of working. As a citizen, I couldn't accept that criminals cared so little about the lives of others as to risk killing innocent people and even children. You don't have to be a genius to know that the explosion of a powerful bomb can wreak havoc in a densely populated neighbourhood.

Following this boy's death, I became even more interested in exploring the underside of this famous biker war. I wrote more articles on its major players, which in turn put me in the hot seat. This series of articles, spread over several years, is what sealed my fate in September 2000. I'd become too much of a nuisance to the lords of this war, a war attributable to some bikers thinking they ruled the world. The thought they could do as they pleased.

Despite all the media hype that followed the death of the Desrochers boy, the Hells Angels pursued their activities. They launched an unprecedented campaign to intimidate police and the authorities. The murder of two prison guards and the attempted murder of a third in 1997 made a great deal of noise for several months. According to testimony heard at Maurice Boucher's first trial, these crimes had a diabolical purpose. The sentence for killing police officers and prison guards, normally twenty-five years, cannot be reduced – the criminal must serve the full term. The loyalty of any biker who committed such a crime was therefore assured: he could not hope to get a reduced sentence by informing against his associates and becoming a Crown witness.

However, with Boucher's acquittal and rise to the status of public figure, the general public quickly forgot the names of the prison guards. During this new biker war, I was again at the forefront of media coverage, which earned us many phone calls and threats. I wrote several articles on the Rockers gang, which had been in Rosemont for many years. This local branch of the Hells Angels haunted certain establishments where *Journal de Montréal* employees were also regulars. So I ran into these bikers. Among those I often met was André Tousignant. He was very close to Angels' senior management, which didn't prevent him from being killed by members of the organization.

From the outset of the gang war, Tousignant, nicknamed Toots, was a sort of spokesman for the bikers. He gave a few interviews and said he earned a living by "selling peanuts." He explained very seriously that motorcycle gangs were groups of friends who occasionally got together at their club to have peace and quiet. "We get away from our wives and kids to play cards." He didn't explain why they needed sophisticated surveillance systems, bulletproof windows and doors, as well as armed guards to protect their building, which was often visited by police.

Later identified as one of the prison-guard assassins, Tousignant was found dead, his body partially burned. His supposed accomplice for a murder, Paul Fontaine, called Fon-fon, is still wanted. Some say he's dead, but his friends claim he's still alive, which certain specialized police believe.

Using all possible municipal regulations, the City of Montreal finally closed down the gang's bunker on Gilford Street. Achieving this, however, required the determination of municipal counsellor Robert Côté, a former senior MUC police officer.

Côté was mostly known for his defusing of bombs in the days of the FLQ.

Previously, on March 21, 1995, I had disclosed that the federal government had provided funds for the bikers to purchase their bunker. The Federal Business Development Bank (FBDB) had agreed to give the Rockers a mortgage to buy the building. Given responsibility for funding small and medium-size businesses by the federal government, the bank has also provided funds to strip clubs.

I was also the one to disclose the creation of the Hells Angels Nomads chapter. The group brought together nine of the gang's leaders. The Nomads were targeted by police investigations for participation in most of the major crimes attributed to the Hells Angels. They were leaders of the war against the Rock Machine and the Alliance, a group of drug traffickers from various backgrounds that the Angels wanted to eliminate.

With each new revelation, bikers were getting angrier. But never did anyone threaten me or send me a violent message. With the war's intensification, crimes attributed to the Hells Angels became more serious and despicable. Several relatively unimportant individuals were killed in the spring of 2000. Some were killed only because they were related to enemies who were on the blacklist.

On returning from summer holidays, I started looking into the files of various murders to see what was really going on in the biker war. Several months previously, the Rock Machine had become Bandidos, the third largest gang in the world, while the Angels were organizing their entry into Ontario, where the new Bandidos had already established a stronghold. The Hells Angels were furious when I wrote that their enemies had been quicker to expand into Ontario.

On September 12, the *Journal de Montréal* published the conclusions of my investigation, where I basically took stock of the latest violence involving bikers and Mafiosos. Those two pages, titled "CHAOS AMONG BOSSES," would be the last I'd write for quite a while.

At the time, I didn't know the Hells Angels were looking for personal information about me, my car, and the places I frequented. I especially didn't know that killers were on my trail. Nor did I know they were watching me and waiting for the right moment to kill me.

The next hours of my life would be very turbulent.

10

A Lost Day

I magine that you're sound asleep and that you suddenly hear unknown voices. That's what happened to me on my hospital bed. A doctor was asking whether I knew the day of the week and where I was. Silly questions! I knew I was in the hospital. It was Wednesday, I'd been shot several times that morning, and was waking up after an obviously successful operation. But I was wrong. It wasn't Wednesday night, as I thought, but Thursday. I'd lost a day.

Very slowly, I opened my eyes and recognized my close relatives, all of them smiling. I gave my daughter a timid smile. Guylaine responded with a heartfelt "I love you." I was returning from very far away, something like being in a dream. After performing the usual checks to make sure I'd come back to reality, the doctor told me the operations had been a success.

That's when I began to understand the seriousness of my injuries and to learn what had happened to me over the last thirty-six hours, a period I had no recollection of. I'd survived the bullets, and the doctors had done a wonderful job. I was alive! I had felt the end was near when the killer shot me. Now I began to realize it was a miracle I'd survived the attack.

It was good to see loved ones at my bedside. But I didn't have much energy and fell asleep. I heard voices as I slept and awakened to find a nurse at the foot of the bed. She told me that I had been very agitated after the two operations and that I had reacted to the words of my loved ones as they stood by.

I was in a large room filled with all kinds of medical devices. There were a lot of comings and goings. My throat was blocked by a large annoying tube. The nurse told me my breathing hadn't returned to normal and that the tube could be removed quickly if I made an effort to breathe deeply. The kind of advice I didn't need to be given twice. I think the tube disappeared an hour later.

During that turbulent night, I realized I was in intensive care, next to the operating room. A sophisticated lab, a factory for saving lives. I'm tempted to say that doctors resurrect people there. Eight patients surrounded me, all of them in very serious condition, people at death's door whom medical staff were calmly trying to revive. The area was under heavy police security to ensure my protection. As a precaution, my name hadn't been officially registered. Even the medical record didn't mention my identity. I was officially anonymous, even if all staff, conscious patients, and visitors knew who I was.

Only on Friday morning did I fully realize what was happening around me. The doctor who visited me briefly explained what the medical team had accomplished over the last two days. I'd been hit by six bullets, and two major operations had been needed to make repairs. The first one had lasted three hours and allowed removal of a bullet that had gone through the colon. Having staunched the hemorrhaging, the medical team had decided to continue the operation the next day. I was anaesthetized and immobilized for twenty-four hours so I could be operated on again to find a bullet that was visible on X-rays but had been impossible to locate.

Another bullet gave doctors much to worry about. It was lodged near the third lumbar vertebra and rested on the spinal chord. On the first day, X-rays and a scan had shown it would be extremely risky to remove it. And to complicate matters, the vertebra was fractured. They also had concluded that other bullets had to be left where they were. One of the projectiles had fractured the seventh cervical vertebra. I was immobilized with a large collar because specialists feared that the injury might lead to paralysis.

A few days later, I saw an X-ray of my new back, improved with the addition of four metal pieces. Besides two fragments of the same bullet located near the spine, another was lodged near the left hip and another near the right shoulder blade. A doctor explained that removing them would be too risky. The human body can live with all kinds of added parts. It seems that a muscular envelope develops around the foreign body that, even though it's lead, won't cause problems later on. "If the bullets move around, we'll still have time to deal with them. For the moment, it's wiser to do nothing." The doctor seemed knowledgeable, so I trusted him. The same day, my colleague Michèle Coudé-Lord wrote an article in the *Journal de Montréal* about the risks of extracting bullets and the disadvantages of living with them inside the body.

I asked whether these bullets would trigger metal detectors in airports. The doctor laughed and told me that, as far as he knew, I'd have no problems going through security checks.

During all this time, my girlfriend, Michèle, who just had spent forty-eight horrible hours in hallways and the intensive care ward, was at my bedside. She listened, spoke little. But, after the doctor left, she told me about all that had happened in the city since the attempt. I'd been a journalist for a long time and knew this news had made a lot of noise, but I never thought the attack would arouse the public to such an extent. Bikers had hoped to silence me, but the total opposite happened. I learned that a march would take place at midday to denounce the attack that was deemed an unacceptable act of intimidation by all journalists and editors.

Suffering physically and under the effect of morphine and other medication, I have forgotten much of what happened in my first day of convalescence. One incident stands out: I was intrigued by an X-ray hanging on the door of intensive care. It showed the lungs and above them a practically straight line. It turned out to be an X-ray of my lungs, with the track of a bullet from one side of the back to the other.

At one point I spotted MUC police chief Michel Sarrazin, one of his immediate assistants, Robert Montanaro, and officer Normand Couillard leaving the intensive care ward practically on tiptoes. I asked another officer nearby to tell the trio of men I wanted to talk to them. The three returned, very surprised to see me. They thought I'd been transferred to another hospital. Sarrazin explained they were here to be at the bedside of one of their colleagues, officer Alain Matte, who had been hospitalized for several weeks as a result of a serious work-related accident. The officer's condition never improved and his death was now imminent.

A little later, I saw the officer's wife and family gather round him for the last time. The chaplain for the police and fire brigade, Jesuit Champlain Barrette, administered last rites. Seeing me as he was leaving, the chaplain came over to comfort me. He informed me as well of the solidarity march and spoke about the widespread indignation. "Many people used to say the biker war wasn't their concern," he said, "but they now realize their mistake."

I didn't get comfort only from religion during those difficult moments. I also got a friendly visit from the Montreal Canadiens' official doctor. My name and wishes for a quick recovery had been posted on the Molson Centre's large scoreboard.

Pierre McCann is my best friend. For more than thirty years, we've worked, travelled, fished, and tinkered about together. Our families did everything together since we met in the *La Presse* newsroom in 1968. Often working as a team, we followed crooks and covered all the large public demonstrations at the time. For two days, Pierre had also been living in the hallways of the emergency ward with Michèle, my daughter, Guylaine, and my younger brother Alain, representing the rest of my family, the others having gathered around my mother, Armande, while awaiting news. They all had difficulty believing what specialists were saying, namely, that I would pull through. The doctors had been very worried in the first hours after my hospitalization, but were more optimistic on the second day, following the second major operation.

On day three of this misadventure, Pierre walked into intensive care and saw that my condition was improving. From the beginning, the journalistic instinct being what it is, Pierre had kept his cameras nearby. You never know when an opportunity might arise.

I encouraged him to take my picture. "You haven't lost your reporter's instinct," he said. He asked the nurse if there were any objections to him taking photographs. Her negative answer didn't surprise us. Hospital management is usually very allergic to journalists and press photographers, but staff, for its part, are used to seeing the families of patients take souvenir photos.

It only took a few seconds to snap twenty or so photographs, which, though very similar, would be used by various media. The goal was to provide a photo to the *Journal de Montréal*, my employer, to *La Presse*, his employer, as well as to the Canadian Press, the agency providing articles and photos to media across the country.

Pierre was greeted joyfully at the march, which took place a little later on Mount Royal Avenue, when he provided friends and colleagues with photographic proof that my condition was improving. Though still very weak and connected to all kinds of devices, it was in the aftermath of this photo session that I really understood how lucky I had been. I had seen people die from a single bullet. How could my killer have missed from such close range? Had his weapon malfunctioned? Why had he left the crime scene without finishing the job he'd been ordered to do?

As for every kind of business, newspapers get their share of memorable days. September 15, 2000, was such a day for employees of the *Journal de Montréal*. The solidarity march brought together employees and managers from every department of the paper, as well as from the printer, all of them united in support of a colleague who'd become a symbol for freedom of the press. André Dalcout, one of the paper's most senior news desk editors, visited me a little later, saying, "This is a big day for the paper. I'm sorry you weren't there." So am I.

Demonstrators, more than a thousand of them, marched behind two large banners. The first one read: "Freedom of the press: an inalienable right." One end was held by journalists' union president Martin Leclerc, the other by news editor Dany Doucet. Also present as standard bearers were Gilles Gougeon, from the CBC; Hélène Pichette, president of the Fédération professionnelle des journalistes du Québec (FPJQ); Marc Laviolette, president of the Confederation of National Trade Unions (CNTU); and Pascale Perrault, a colleague and former president of our union. Also attending was Jean-Pierre Charbonneau, my former student, colleague, and competitor who'd become an elected member of the Parti Québécois and at this time was

Speaker of the Quebec National Assembly. Jean-Pierre also had been the victim of an attack.

One day, while in *Le Devoir*'s newsroom, then located on Saint-Sacrement Street, Jean-Pierre was the target of a Mafia henchman. "Are you Charbonneau?" the unknown man had asked. Following an affirmative answer, the man pulled out a gun and fired. Jean-Pierre was hit by a bullet in the forearm. The gunman had aimed for the journalist's head, but Jean-Pierre, protecting himself by falling to the ground, made him miss.

Another former journalist, who plied his trade part-time, was discreetly walking at the back of the group of demonstrators. Robert Monastesse was a freelancer who occasionally wrote articles for *La Presse* as a special contributor. He also wrote about bikers, the Rock Machine especially. In February 1995, an unknown man showed up at his doorstep in Laval and shot him in the legs. Police didn't quite know what to make of this unusual attack and the inquiry led nowhere. Later, specialized police included this attack in the list of intimidation tactics attributed to biker gangs. Monastesse has not written since the time he was attacked. Unlike me, he worked practically on his own. He wasn't lucky enough to work for an established paper and to have a solid network of contacts and friends in various fields.

The other banner, "No to Intimidation," was carried by photographer André Viau, journalist Michel Marsolais, and news desk officer Jean-Marie Bertrand. I didn't get to hear the brilliant speech given by Paule Beaugrand-Champagne in the *Journal de Montréal* parking lot, where someone had tried to kill me a little more than forty-eight hours earlier. I was later told that, during that speech, my friend McCann was standing exactly where I had been shot.

However, I did read an account of Beaugrand-Champagne's speech in the paper. My boss had said the march had been held not only for a journalist, "but for the innocent public threatened by people who want to take control of our society." She also said, "Our duty is to inform the public to give it the means to pressure governments to change specific laws to ensure that criminal groups end up where they belong, behind bars." Beaugrand-Champagne then mentioned the numerous news items we read each day, often forgetting that these events affect families and innocent people. She concluded by emphasizing that I'd always tried to report facts, that I'd never forgotten people touched by tragedies. In trying to explain things, my boss said, I had put myself in danger. She also recalled that I did my job with passion. For his part, the president of the Conseil de presse du Québec, Michel Roy, said that an attack on one journalist was an attack on the entire profession.

When I saw photographs of the demonstration, I noticed that Pierre McCann's face was beaming and that he appeared to be relieved at the turn of events. This was his second great misfortune in less than a year. On October 31, 1999, we'd lost two mutual friends: Jeannine Bourdages and Claude Masson. They were travelling to Egypt aboard EgyptAir Flight 990 when it crashed into the Atlantic off Massachusetts, with its 217 passengers.

The day after the march, my colleague Bertrand Raymond wrote the following in his column in the *Journal de Montréal*'s sports section.

A COLLEAGUE'S OLYMPICS

Walking Is an Olympic Discipline.
    At the Barcelona Games, the Quebec press had delighted in the exploit of the amiable Guillaume Leblanc, silver medalist in the twenty-kilometre walk.
    Guillaume had suffered a great deal from the heat, which was amplified by humidity, to get Canada's first Olympic

walking medal in eighty years. He suffered physically and, in a way, mentally, since, back home, in Rimouski, awaiting her second child, his wife Manon was at the edge of contractions in front of her TV.

Our march along Mount Royal Avenue yesterday wasn't Olympian. It was a simple physical exercise spread over some twenty street corners. Not enough to wind journalists used to toiling comfortably seated at their computers.

This was an exercise in solidarity. We were marching out of friendship for a courageous man, a humble colleague who, transformed into a colander by a gangster, is now competing in his own Olympics.

The Exploit of a Lifetime

I remember the headline on the *Journal de Montréal*'s front page following Leblanc's hard-won medal: "The Exploit of a Lifetime," the athlete had shouted. For Michel Auger, the exploit of a lifetime means hanging on to his life.

Men's Olympic walking consists of two events: the twenty- and fifty-kilometre races. Yesterday morning, when Auger managed to talk to his girlfriend for the first time and learned about how much people had worried about him since the shooting, he had the reflex of a professional. He asked his old buddy, photographer Pierre McCann, to take a snapshot of him to inform people that his aggressors hadn't knocked him down for the count.

For that gesture alone, he won gold in the twenty kilometres. The next race will lead him to a complete recovery and take the form of an endurance test.

Rekindled Fervour

He might one day tell his grandson, now three-years old, and his granddaughter, to be born in a month, that he survived the worst of aggressions, a barbaric attack which compelled all of Quebec to wave the flag of democracy with unusual fervour.

When we talk about freedom of the press, democracy often takes the form of a simple cliché. We talk about it as something that's been acquired and which it's useless to protect or defend.

We don't think it's threatened til the day an incorruptible colleague, who felt protected by his press pass, is felled by a hail of gunfire.

We marched in grey, cool weather to defend the right to information and to express our moral support for Michel Auger, as did those who transformed his office into a touching bed of multicoloured flowers.

Good thing the weather was a little dreary. The march was no picnic. It provided a moment to reflect on this profession we love so much, which sometimes entails certain risks.

It would have been almost indecent for the sun to shine while the friend who inspired the rally nurses his wounds inside a rather gloomy room. A room which came back to life, as it were, since he started to communicate again. You see his mocking smile on the photo gracing this page. That's exactly who Michel Auger is.

Medalist on the Front Page

That's the smile he sported daily in this room. It was impossible to discern the threats that tormented him and made him go grey prematurely.

While the march was drawing to a close in the parking lot where he'd nearly breathed his last, my colleague Michèle Coudé-Lord is the one who best summed up the effect Auger has over us: "A happy chatterbox we love and feel like having a coffee with."

If he had strength to watch TV yesterday, Michel Auger likely felt appreciated.

I wish he could've seen people waving from their windows and on their balconies, during this respectful march.

As an Olympian behind the day's feat of arms, he's entitled to the front page.

Auger is a grandfather, but he'll never practice stale journalism. A gold medallist of guts in the journalism Olympics.

Time crawls by when you're lying on a hospital bed, even if everything is fine and there is cause for optimism. I was gradually learning about all that had happened while I'd been unconscious. Doctors and staff were lavishing attention on me. I very quickly realized that my desire to remain anonymous was far from being fulfilled.

When I came to, I was made to sit, with great difficulty, in a chair beside my bed in intensive care. Then, after three days in the hospital, I was transferred to a regular room. I was still pretty weak when I took my first steps towards the bathroom. The first time I left my room to walk down the hall with a serum bag on a rolling intravenous pole, visitors and patients in adjoining rooms saluted as though I were an acquaintance. It must be said that my room, located at the end of the hall, was conspicuous with two police officers constantly guarding my door, along with staff hired by the *Journal de Montréal* to ensure the safety of my close relatives.

As soon as I was able to answer questions, investigators and their supervisors came to see me. I wasn't very helpful, since I was unable to recognize my aggressor. Though I'd tried to remember the face of the man who wanted to kill me, I couldn't. Nor could I recall any peculiar event or any suspect vehicle I might have seen the morning of the attack.

I was also surprised to discover I felt no hostility towards the killer or his accomplices, nor even towards those I fully suspected of having ordered them to murder me. I often wondered whether anyone besides the bikers could resent me to the point they'd want to kill me.

Every morning the entire medical team appeared to carry out its daily inspection. Dr. Tarek Razek and his colleague Patrick Charlebois are the ones who asked me most of the questions. They were surrounded by interns who were looking for as much information as possible on my condition. I began to understand that my condition was, if not unique, then pretty rare.

Some of my visitors talked about the miracle of my survival. One of my bosses took to calling me a "living legend." He even jokingly suggested my file be sent to the *Guinness Book of World Records*. It isn't usual for a journalist to survive a volley of gunfire, to have four bullets still in his body, and to continue smiling.

I received hundreds of messages of sympathy and the police carefully checked all packages or gifts arriving in my room. Since the details of my temporary address weren't known, some gifts, including an immense basket of fruit and other delights, were sent to the police station. The wine bottle passed with no problem, but the fruit was inspected by the technical squad, who were looking for bombs or other such gadgets. All the same, some of the fruit was rescued from the inspectors – and eaten!

$$\boxed{11}$$

Two Weeks to Ponder

I spent two weeks and a day in that hospital, undergoing three operations. The third one was to rework the long scar on my stomach created as a result of internal repairs and the extraction of two bullets. Each day, nurses bandaged my wounds and stuffed me with antibiotics. Doctors feared I had caught a virus inside the hospital. I had a lot of time to think about the circumstances surrounding the attack, about the security measures I was taking, and, finally, about what I'd do when they sent me home.

The McGill University Hospital Centre is located halfway up Mount Royal, and, from my room, I could see the St. Lawrence River, mountains on the south shore, and a little of the countryside. The vista revived old dreams of building a log cabin, a small sap house, a place I could share with my three-year-old grandson, Nicholas, and his little sister, Amélie, who'd be born in less than a month if all went according to plan.

I mused about the good moments in my career, as well as the others. My professional life had been very full and I felt I'd accomplished most of my goals, at least the ones that were accessible to me. That's why the idea of retirement was starting to seem attractive. Following the attack, who could blame me for wanting to leave this job? I was worried about my attackers, who were surely disappointed at having failed, and I was uneasy about returning to work, to the life I had known.

I was also beginning to discover some unexpected effects of the attempt on my life. Additional money was being allocated to police forces. New laws were being prepared. Files that had been gathering dust in certain ministries were brought back to the forefront. I was even told that some judges had changed their attitude about the files of certain criminals. The bikers would surely regret having attacked a journalist.

On September 13, 2000, criminals had tried to silence me and had briefly succeeded. But my bosses and colleagues at the *Journal de Montréal* had understood that we couldn't yield to intimidation. Biker activities have been covered prominently since then. Other media have also given renewed attention to the crooks' criminal activities. The Hells Angels expansion into Ontario had also enhanced the information campaign in the province on bikers and their drug trafficking.

The attempt to kill me prompted the indignation not only of journalists across the country, but of police and politicians as well. Moreover, use of more radical means to fight criminal biker gangs became an important issue in the fall 2000 federal election campaign. While the Bloc Québécois constantly requested the strengthening of measures to deal with gangs and organized crime, Liberal MPs, who were in power, seemed to think everything was just fine. Only when they were returned to power did the Liberals change their attitude and propose more severe methods for going after organized criminals.

The death of a young bar owner in Terrebonne, north of Montreal, also gave more arguments to those who thought our laws were too lax. Francis Laforest had refused to allow Hells

Angels drug pushers access to his establishment. He was killed with baseball bats. This death lead my boss, Serge Labrosse, to write a hard-hitting article in the *Journal de Montréal*. Who'd march in the streets for Francis Laforest? When I found out a march was being organized to denounce this heinous violence, I decided to take part. I was constantly surrounded by two sturdy fellows, who'd also come to participate in the solidarity march. More than two thousand of us gathered in the usually quiet streets of that municipality on a beautiful October Saturday.

The banner that had denounced intimidation during the march towards the *Journal de Montréal* offices, two days following the attempt to kill me, saw renewed action. This time, I was there with my colleagues and bosses to march with Francis Laforest's family and friends. When I went over to offer condolences to the Laforest family, I felt a little embarrassed. I was ill at ease climbing the stairs of the funeral home. How would they greet me, since I'd been shot by a volley of bullets five weeks earlier and had miraculously survived? Their son hadn't been so lucky. He was lying there, beneath the tear-filled gazes of his loved ones. But the young man's parents said they appreciated that all these ordinary citizens, politicians, and journalists had come to demonstrate against this absurd violence.

For more than thirty years, I've regularly gotten all kinds of threats. I've been told I'd be killed, my car blown up, my house destroyed. But until September 13, 2000, nothing had happened. A few years ago, the garage mechanic repairing a flat tire on my car exclaimed with surprise when he found a bullet in it. I've kept that bullet as a souvenir and a recent expert opinion confirmed what I'd thought at the time: the bullet hadn't been fired from a gun. But such a discovery is perplexing when you're a journalist who constantly denounces major crime bosses.

Some of them weren't very fond of me. I was nearly always present when Frank Cotroni was arrested over major drug trafficking in Canada and the United States. Cotroni and his right-hand man at the time had commented on the length of my legs, hinting that he intended to shorten them for me. I was a very young journalist and I needed my legs – both of them – to take me from the offices of *La Presse*, where I worked to the courthouse across the street. Cotroni was at the height of his power when he was sent to be tried in New York. However, his position as lieutenant of the Montreal Mafia, then headed by his older brother, Vincent, didn't prevent him from going to jail.

In March 1996, in the midst of the biker war, I was advised by leaders of the Wolverine squad that criminals were seriously seeking confidential information about me. The threat was so serious that police officers asked that I immediately leave my home and spend the weekend in a hotel. The following Monday, I met two senior officers, one from the MUC police, the other from the QPF, who informed me about the danger. A certain Hells Angels leader felt his photo was published a little too often in the *Journal de Montréal*.

After a week of travelling from one hotel to the next, I was able to resume my normal life. Meanwhile, police had raided the bikers' headquarters, solving two cases pertaining to the intimidation of journalists at once. Besides looking into my private life, the bikers had threatened my colleague Gaétan Girouard, a reporter with the TVA network at the time. Bikers had taken a sudden dislike to Girouard, who later committed suicide, even trying to run him out of Sorel during the funeral of one of their members.

I'd always thought that bikers could attack my car, but never imagined my life was in real danger. I settled for taking certain precautions when leaving the office or public areas whenever I published an article likely to make waves. Moreover, I wasn't afraid when Maurice Boucher or his friends, like Robert Savard who was recently murdered, gave me rather clear verbal messages. But the attempt clearly proved I'd been wrong. At the end of my hospitalization and during the ten or so days I then spent in another place under good protection, ideas jostled in my head. How would I undertake my new life? I'd promised my family that never again would my work put them through such stress.

I got in touch with several acquaintances and friends from every milieu. This information search allowed me to discover that those who'd tried to kill me would bitterly regret their gesture. The entire criminal field was furious. Why provoke such a public debate, and such an offensive from the forces of law and order. Intelligent criminals avoid that kind of confrontation.

A criminal imprisoned for a series of crimes, including particularly heinous murders, apprised me of his indignation. "What they've done to you is disgusting," he said, asking if he could "help." I simply asked him to contact police officers in charge of the investigation if he knew anything that could lead to the identification and sentencing of the would-be killers.

Other informers and ordinary people, readers, also provided help by phoning me or giving police details and information, some of which turned out to be very valuable.

That's the backdrop against which I was planning to retire. But I quickly changed my mind. I feel, and many people share this view, that, since the attempt was botched, the criminals now consider the case closed.

For a while, I decided to shun a certain type of reporting, so that I wouldn't be in a conflict of interest and to avoid uselessly provoking those who tried to kill me.

I'd entered the hospital through the door to the emergency ward and left through that of the morgue. Alive, of course. For security reasons, the team escorting me had chosen this discreet exit. In the first moments of my return to normal life, I decided to surprise my colleagues by visiting them at the newspaper.

I thought I could return to the parking lot where I'd been shot, then enter the newsroom by the small back door, with neither noise nor fuss. But things didn't go as I'd planned. Security measures were very tight when we reached the newspaper's offices and there was no way the escort could enter anywhere else but through the main door, where my bosses were waiting for me. Only a few people had been advised of my visit. Very quickly, however, people surrounded and embraced me. Since I was still weak, someone got me a chair, and it's inside a large circle of friends and colleagues that I understood how much all these folks had been afraid for me. During two weeks, the paper's entire team, not only my newsroom colleagues, but all employees in the building had only had one conversation topic: my health and the great luck I'd had.

They began by asking me personal questions, wanting to know everything, then telling me how happy they were to see me. I also discovered I'd become a news celebrity. A TVA journalist was already at the door asking for an interview. He understood my need for tranquility and accepted my decision not to grant it.

I then spent ten days in a hotel surrounded by security. That's where I realized that my life had changed. This was when former prime minister Pierre Elliott Trudeau had died. Alone in a hotel room, you have a lot of time to think. A television program is what gave me the first real test to determine if the attempt would leave me with psychological scars. I was watching an old gangster film where someone hidden in a closet half-opened the door, pointing a pistol equipped with a silencer, a weapon like the one used on me fifteen days previously. My first reflex was to change the channel. But I changed my mind in a second. I heard the gunshots, saw blood spurt from the victim, but was surprised to feel no fear.

I'd thereby discover I was practically immune to fear. A few days later, while in the offices of the homicide squad, I was again able to test my mental condition in the wake of September 13. I was talking about the moments that had followed the attempt with the two main investigators working on my file. When I said I was no longer really sure what I'd said to the 911 operator when I'd sent my SOS, Guy Bessette offered to give me a second test. After looking his partner, Michel Whissel, in the eyes, he turned around and said, "Nothing's easier than listening to that message if you want. The cassette's in the file." I immediately accepted the offer. I'd thought about asking to listen to this recording, but since I wasn't sure of my reaction, I'd simply put off that request.

The two investigators had set up their quarters in a conference room, having accumulated fifteen or so cases of documents and various reports since they opened the file. Walls in the room were papered with photos of the crime scene, aerial pictures, and topographic maps. On it as well were the two pages of articles published the day before the attempt, and the famous photo from intensive care. Police had also placed a photo taken in Paris of three gendarmes and I at the door to the hôtel des Invalides. I'd teasingly given them this souvenir, writing, "Hope you're still working hard while I'm away from Montreal."

Bessette was having trouble locating the desired tape, which gave me time to think, since I was no longer sure I really wanted to hear that conversation. Still, I was a little afraid of my reaction. What would it be? With his trademark irony, Bessette asked if I was ready, if I really wanted to listen to the tape. I said yes, without showing my apprehension. He pressed the button, but the wrong cassette was in the machine.

On second try, it was the right recording:

Recording of Call no. 000913-022
Related to Event 38-000913-019

Montreal Urban Community Police Department (MUCPD):
    MUC police 236

911: Hello, Urgences-Santé . . . with the police.

MUCPD: Yes, hello.

A: Listen, I've been shot.

MUCPD: Where?

A: At the *Journal de Montréal*.

MUCPD: At what address?

A: 4545 Frontenac.

MUCPD: 4545 Frontenac.

A: In the south parking lot.

MUCPD: Okay. Stay on the line, sir, I'm sending you help, the
    ambulance and firemen.

A: Not to make conversation, surely.

MUCPD: Parking lot?

A: South.

MUCPD: South. Who shot you?

A: I don't know, an armed man who headed towards the
    Angus shops.

MUCPD: Okay. Towards the Angus shops.

A: (breathing.)

MUCPD: Did you see the man?

A: Listen, listen, lady, I didn't see a thing.

MUCPD: You didn't see a thing.

A: I saw a guy with a weapon and all that, and I don't even
    know if I'm bleeding. I'm in pain and that's it.

MUCPD: Okay. The ambulance and the police are on the way.
    Was the man you saw white or black?

A: I think he was white.

MUCPD: Maybe white. Wearing dark clothing?

A: Dark with a cap.

MUCPD: Armed with a gun?

A: No. A revolver or . . . um . . . a revolver.

MUCPD: Do you work for the press?

A: I'm a journalist, lady. Stop talking to me.

MUCPD: Your name.

A: Michel Auger.

MUCPD: Mr. Auger.

A: I cover biker gangs for the paper.

MUCPD: Okay, Mr. Auger. The police and ambulance are on
the way. Are you in the parking lot?

A: Yes.

MUCPD: All right. Is someone there helping you?

A: No one's here. No one's seen me.

MUCPD: Is it a large parking lot?

A: Yes.

MUCPD: Okay. Your number?

A: My car's right in the entrance.

MUCPD: What kind of vehicle?

A: The door . . . a Subaru. The door's open.

MUCPD: Near what colour of Subaru vehicle?

A: Brown

MUCPD: Brown. Your cell phone number?

After giving her my number, I simply ended the conversation. I had other things to do . . .

My heart was racing as I listened to the recording and heard my voice. I sounded out of breath and seemed a little tired, contrary to the recollection that was etched into my memory. I thought my voice had been calm and clear as usual. The young woman's questions were coming back to me. As I was listening, I felt neither fear nor stress. I was afterwards happy to have listened to the cassette and, especially, relieved about my reaction.

Following my release from hospital, my bosses called on psychologist Jacques Lamarre, who oversees the employee assistance program. All my friends and colleagues and, of course, my close relatives worried about my psychological reactions. They could plainly see I was on the right path physically; however, they were worried about my capacity to resume a normal life. I often repeated that I wasn't afraid and that I'd go back to living as I had before, while making a few adjustments. Many people were telling me to take my time, to take it easy. They were trying to encourage me.

I'd had time to analyze my reactions and was sure I had no deeply rooted malaise, but I agreed to meet the psychologist. Ginette Soucy told me that few people experience a trauma like the one I had been through without suffering after-effects. I was apparently one of the rare cases, and can still live my life without being afraid of going out or working. Soucy, however, did warn me that this tranquility might one day be interrupted. A gunshot, an ordinary gesture in a parking lot, or seeing certain things that would remind me of circumstances surrounding the attempt might trouble me. I shouldn't be surprised if the fateful moment returned to haunt me. But the psychologist also said reassuring things. She observed that I had asked myself all the right questions and suggested that I was on the right track. For myself, I'm not worried.

|12|

Tributes

The outpouring of support from ordinary people astonished me. On my very first outing, I went to a Duluth Street restaurant to have lunch with my three bosses, Serge Labrosse, Dany Doucet, and Paule Beaugrand-Champagne. No sooner had I set foot on the street than a van stopped and the driver, a florist's delivery man, wished me the best of luck. The restaurant we chose was Le Jardin de Panos, a fashionable brochetterie and the first of its kind in Quebec. The owner recognized me and offered us lunch on the house, while his wife gave us a friendly smile.

On that day, Doucet offered me a management job, which I immediately turned down. "I was shot in the back, but I haven't fallen on my head!" I answered.

Friendly comments from the public have never ceased. I learned of only one hostile message. It was from a man saying my bosses had made everything up to sell more papers and that I was a bastard for going along with the game. However, most other people saluted me with a smile. Some came over to congratulate me, others simply wanted to shake my hand. Many people praised my courage and denounced the useless criminal violence.

On November 2, I was invited to Quebec City's National Assembly. I received tributes from Premier Lucien Bouchard, from Opposition Leader Jean Charest, and from Action Démocratique Leader Mario Dumont. I don't recall many times when this large assembly displayed such wonderful unanimity. I was embarrassed to listen to all this praise about my work and personal qualities. It was a bit like hearing tributes at my own funeral.

Bouchard underscored my courage and my "refusal to remain silent." "Last September 13, the news brutally reminded us how vulnerable we are," he said. Charest said he was "saluting a hero who had the courage to say, write and denounce certain things." Dumont spoke of the need to protect fundamental democratic principles. "Special measures must be taken every time any type of free expression is threatened," he said. Earlier, in private, Charest told me I had the makings of a politician. He said this after hearing me evade questions from political journalists attending the awarding of the National Assembly's medal.

In answering one of those questions I accidentally made everyone guffaw. A reporter asked if I had any advice for young journalists who might want to follow my career path. My answer, in a humorous tone, consisted of a few general tips and I ended by saying you should never let anyone cut you down. I immediately apologized for the play on words. That night, TV newscasts reported the event and naturally highlighted that part of my statement.

This ceremony was a very important event in my life. My friend Jean-Pierre Charbonneau, then Speaker of the National Assembly, awarded me the rarely given National Assembly medal in the presence of my entire family. Jean-Pierre is the only student I ever had in my thirty-seven-year career. He was an intern with *La Presse* in 1970 and spent several months with me. Shortly thereafter, he became my competitor at *Le Devoir*.

He had absolutely no compunction about using the tricks I'd taught him. The competition was intense for a few years, but we always remained good friends. In 1976, for only a few months, we again worked together for *La Presse*. But he preferred politics and was part of the Parti Québécois team carried to power in November 1976. The attempt against me awoke bad memories for Jean-Pierre. Like me, he had been shot, in his case when he was only twenty-three.

Accompanied by my family, I had a brief private meeting with the premier. He was delighted to see my granddaughter, Amélie, who was barely two weeks old. He was to retire two months later and observed that he missed his own children. The meeting with Bouchard ended when a photo was taken for posterity. The whole family, with Bouchard, Charbonneau, and Nicolet MNA Michel Morin, who happens to be a relative, was smiling broadly. My boss, Serge Labrosse, is very tall. Being discreet, he placed himself at the back of the group, and only the top of his face is visible.

A few days later, I received a hand-written letter from Bernard Landry, who was soon to replace Bouchard. He wrote the following: "Now that the tide of messages and honours you so richly deserved and received is likely to be waning, I want to convey my admiration for the courage and competence you display in the exercise of your profession. Journalism produces the best and worst, and it seems that the worst is what has scored points over the last few years. Clearly, you incarnate the best. Your profession is a cornerstone of freedom and democracy, and I want to thank and congratulate you for what you do for us."

In many countries, journalism is a dangerous profession. The World Association of Newspapers recently reported that fifty-three journalists and media professionals were killed around the world in 2000. We journalists can console ourselves that this number was lower than the previous year, when seventy-five colleagues were killed worldwide. Colombia and Russia have been among the most dangerous countries, but events can make many localities dangerous.

When I was taking my first steps as a young journalist in the newsroom of *Le Nouvelliste* in Shawinigan, I never imagined I'd become a symbol for the defence of free expression in the world. On November 23, precisely two months following the attempt, the Canadian Journalists for Free Expression (CJFE) awarded me the Tara Singh Hayer Prize to highlight my "important contribution to the reinforcement and defence of the principle of free expression in Canada."

This prize was awarded the previous year to the family of journalist Tara Singh Hayer, murdered in Vancouver in November 1998. This man, the publisher of the *Indo-Canadian Times*, was killed ten years following a first attack that had left him paralyzed. In fall 2000, the RCMP charged an individual over the 1988 attack on Hayer. The same individual is also accused of plotting to blow up the Air India plane that crashed into the Atlantic off the coast of Ireland in 1985, killing 329 people.

The committee that awarded me the prize wanted to underline that my journalistic work was the most difficult and dangerous in Canada and that I'd not only written an important article but followed the issue in a detailed manner for many years. Jan Wong, a *Globe and Mail* reporter and committee member, wrote of my work: "Even in a democracy like Canada, there are limits to freedom of the press and we depend on journalists like Auger to surpass those limits."

The same evening, before some six hundred personalities from Canadian media and politics, the CJFE also handed out its international awards. An Iranian journalist and a young Colombian woman were honoured. Akbar Ganji is a journalist

imprisoned in Tehran for having denounced the Iranian government's involvement in the operations of death squads. Besides
holding journalists, the Iranian government has closed thirty
publications and arrested twenty other journalists opposed to
the fundamentalist regime. Ganji is the best known and most
outspoken of the protesters.

The other recipient, seated beside me at the gala, was
Jineth Bedoya Lima, a twenty-seven-year-old journalist with
El Espectador, a Bogota daily. Bedoya, who covers military activities, was kidnapped, beaten, and sexually assaulted in May
2000 while doing her job following a prison riot. After only a
few months' rest, the young woman went back to work covering
the civil war that has ravaged her country.

The life of Colombian journalists is far from being restful.
In one decade, forty-four journalists were killed and thirty-three
others kidnapped. *El Espectador* is often taken to task for its
aggressive reporting on events related to the civil war, drug
trafficking, and the government's handling of those problems.
In 1986, the paper's editor was murdered by drug traffickers,
and three years later the newsroom was destroyed by a powerful
bomb placed by the Medellín cartel.

Following the Toronto ceremony, I took the plane to
Edmonton to attend two meetings, one at the *Edmonton Sun*
with management and fellow journalists, the other with the
Canadian Association of Journalists. That's where I learned that
CBC reporter Eldred Savoie absolutely wanted to speak to me.
He left a number where I could reach him in Paris.

Because of the eight-hour time difference, I had to wake up
in the middle of the night that Sunday. Savoie told me on the
phone that the Union internationale des journalistes et de la
presse de langue française (UIJPLF)* had placed my name on the

---

* The International Union of French Language Journalists and Press.

list of candidates for the Prix de la libre expression, which it was about to award. "Can you be in Paris tomorrow?" Savoie asked. I left Montreal Tuesday night after receiving official confirmation from the UIJPLF secretary general, Georges Gros. I spent fifty eventful hours in Paris.

When he announced the award of the Prix de la libre expression, Gros said, "Mr. Auger works in conditions that clearly demonstrate that journalists don't only show courage and tenacity in war, but do so as well in urban settings, where dedicated reporters are subjected to intimidation." This prize honours those who "maintain the independence of their publications in difficult environments and against all odds, despite pressures or attacks on their installations or persons." The award was presented to me by the secretary of the francophonie, Boutros Boutros-Ghali, the former UN secretary general.

The end of 2000 would bring more surprises, including that of having my name on the list of people who made significant contributions over the past year. The Canadian Press is a news service that provides photos and articles to various media throughout the country. At the end of each year, it polls its members and draws up a list of people and events featured in the headlines. A few politicians always top the list, but in 2000 the death of former prime minister Pierre Trudeau was the nearly unanimous first choice, obtaining seventy-five votes. Jean Chrétien got twenty-five. Maurice Richard, a star for several generations of hockey fans, who died during the year, got three votes, the same number I did – I still can't believe my eyes or ears. Justin Trudeau, whose eulogy deeply moved thousands of people at his father's funeral, obtained three and a half votes. The great novelist Margaret Atwood obtained two votes, and Izzy Asper, the press magnate, got only one.

At the end of 2000, I was surprised to be asked for an interview by the *Globe and Mail*'s Katherine Ashenburg. "My boss," she told me, "has just reached mid-life and wants to know every-thing that people in the same boat are planning for the rest of their days." Her article, published on the last day of the year, featured the ideas of six "prominent Canadians." People inter-viewed included actress Mary Walsh, who brought humour to the report, and Toronto financier and art collector Bruce Bailey, who talked about his passion for cooking and his desire to have Canadian artists known internationally. Alberta NDP Leader Pam Barrett was also among those asked for their opinions and ideas. She nearly died following an allergic reaction that took place while she was at her dentist's, an event that prompted her to start writing her spiritual autobiography. Writer Alberto Manguel and radio host Shelagh Rogers were also featured in the report.

For my part, I mentioned how much I'd recently been affected by the loss of two friends in the 1999 EgyptAir crash. I also talked about my retirement plan: the building of a small sap house to enjoy with relatives and friends, and especially with my grandchildren. A traditional cabin, far from the city. A cabin with no power, built at the back of the wooded lot I've owned for twenty years. Made using my own trees, which I'll soon start cutting down, then saw into beams and boards.

I've dreamt of this cabin in the middle of the forest for years. Spoken words are fleeting and written ones stay only briefly on people's minds. A well laid-out small wood lot with narrow paths and a small rustic cabin would be, in contrast, a visible and tangible achievement.

In January 2001, less than four months after the attempt on my life, I went back to my regular work schedule. I did interviews and followed certain investigative files that were of particular interest to me. One file that I'd heard about for months concerned a major investigation of several individuals suspected of being closely linked to the attempt. I couldn't wait to find out police secrets. I knew the inquiry was of a scale rarely seen in Quebec.

My first article after going back to work was mostly to thank my *Journal de Montréal* colleagues and all the people who'd sent messages of encouragement. I talked to my boss, Dany Doucet, about getting a little more space. In a daily newspaper, editorial space is often limited, given the abundance of news, and we're forced to keep articles to a certain length. However, as old journalists used to say, it's easier to write a long article than a short one.

And then the holiday season was upon us. The news was very slow and now my boss told me I could have a lot more space. This allowed me to write a full page to relate what had happened and, especially, say why I was going back to work. I explained that I still felt the need to write, to explore hot issues and discover what was really happening in the city. I was too young to retire and wouldn't consider a new career. Journalism is all I know.

My new notoriety brought requests to meet other victims of crime. I was also asked to give speeches on various aspects of organized crime to journalists, police officers, and lawyers. My misadventure took me to various corners of Canada and the United States that I never thought I would visit. I was even invited to give a speech at the annual conference of the Quebec association of psychiatrists. Though I always imagined I might someday have to consult a psychiatrist, I never though that a hundred-odd psychiatrists would consult me.

I was also asked to do publicity concerning some illnesses affecting men, such as erectile dysfunction. I was flattered but couldn't accept these offers, since journalism and publicity are professions that must remain at arm's length.

One day, my colleague Monique Girard-Solomita informed

me that the attempt on my life had been mentioned in an episode of *Virginie*, a CBC soap opera written by Fabienne Larouche. One character, giving advice to another, a cultural journalist who dreams of being an investigative reporter, said, "Be careful, it's dangerous. Look at what happened to Michel Auger." "It's an important day when they talk about you in a soap opera," said my colleague Suzanne Gauthier, the former television reporter with the *Journal de Montréal*.

I got another prestigious award on May 3, 2001, in Toronto. The National Newspaper Awards decided to underscore my "exceptional contribution to journalism." The board of governors had created a special prize that I was the first to receive. On accepting the prize, I was told it was given only in exceptional circumstances. I was particularly moved to see some five hundred colleagues give me a standing ovation during the ceremony. A rare tribute for a colleague. One which seemed to last forever.

On the gold-coloured plaque, an inscription says that this prize is awarded for the first time "to Michel Auger for exemplary journalism. With no consideration for his personal safety, Michel Auger displayed conviction, courage and heroism by informing *Journal de Montréal* readers about developments related to the activities of criminal biker gangs in Quebec."

Now that I have returned to work, I am often asked about my health – naturally. Some journalists thought I had survived because I wore a bullet-proof vest. I'm still laughing over that notion because, had I worn such a vest, I'd have avoided a long period of suffering. I have six holes in my back to show I was only wearing an ordinary cotton shirt on that fateful September day.

Before the attempt on my life, I had booked a holiday in Mexico through a travel agency. I was so sure I'd be going on that trip that I declined to take the usual cancellation insurance. So I spent a month, from the end of January to the end of February, exploring the Mexican countryside before really returning to work.

The following month, I was the first journalist to disclose the secrets of Operation Spring 2001, which targeted the Hells Angels. On March 29, I was particularly proud of my newspaper, since it provided the best coverage of the first exclusive revelations produced by this operation. As a result of this initiative, forty-three bikers were jailed, and collectively face charges for 213 murders. The scale of this investigation was unprecedented in Canada. I had written five articles, including one giving the particulars on how police had been able to record a biker "mass," a meeting where gang leaders make decisions.

More than 135 bikers were arrested altogether. In addition to the forty-three charged with murder, another ninety-two were picked up across the province for drug trafficking and gang-related activities. The following week, a bill designed to reinforce sections of the Criminal Code on organized crime was tabled in Parliament. Police criticized the bill for not going far enough, while some civil libertarians felt it would be abusive. However, as a result of this new legislation, many crooks now understand the scope of the Criminal Code's anti-gang measures. Many citizens claiming to respect the law, but who previously closed their eyes by doing so-called honest business with people who made fortunes from crime, are beginning to fear the new law. Money laundering is also a crime covered by sections of the code dealing with gangsterism.

An undoubted result of the attempt on my life has been an expanded war against gangsters. And the police have been able to use resources and laws in this war that were not previously available to them. Some of the results of this great investigation into biker activities are the subject of the next chapter.

The Biker Who Became a Celebrity

C riminals are usually discreet about their activities. However, for several months in the summer of 2000, Quebec's
best-known biker, Maurice Boucher, had made a number of
public gestures that would set him apart from other characters
in the business. That summer the Quebec Superior Court had
found him not guilty of murdering two prison guards. Following
his triumphant exit from the Montreal courthouse, Boucher
was seen everywhere. He was seen at a televised boxing event.
When he made other court appearances, he'd swagger for the
cameras. He seemed to revel in his new role as a media celebrity.

When one of his friends with the Nomads chapter got
married, Boucher was master of ceremonies. Singer Ginette
Reno and singer-songwriter Jean-Pierre Ferland were photographed singing for the leaders of the most active biker gang in
Canada. Journalists with the weekly *Allô-Police* had been invited
to the wedding to take and then publish photographs staged by
the bikers.

The groom was René Charlebois, nicknamed Baloune, a
tough who quickly made his mark and climbed the various rungs

required to reach the top of the gang's hierarchy. Charlebois was a member of the "Table of Nine," the organization that, according to police, makes all major decisions for the Angels in their campaign against the Bandidos.

Another Table of Nine member, Normand Robitaille, was also at the wedding, accompanied by his wife, a member of the Quebec bar and maid of honour to the young bride. When he was imprisoned with forty-two of his fellow bikers, on March 28, 2001, Robitaille claimed he was unable to defend himself against the murder charges because he hadn't been able to find a lawyer.

Boucher, according to documents given to the bikers charged with murder, is also thought to be one of the heads of the Table of Nine.

Police are now accusing members of this famous Table of Nine of being the leaders in the war that has raged since 1995 between the Hells Angels and their enemies, the Rock Machine, who have since become the Bandidos. At the outset of hostilities, the Hells Angels' enemies were various drug traffickers united within the Alliance, a group that is part of the Rock Machine, the other important organization in Quebec.

Following broadcast of the wedding photos, which were greeted with derision by many of Quebec's public personalities, Boucher continued his public-relations campaign by sending a photo of himself with former premier Robert Bourassa to *Allô-Police*. The bikers had been trying for months to have that photo published. The *Journal de Montréal*, among others, had decided not to use it. It came about when Bourassa, years ago stopped at a small restaurant in the Sorel region, had agreed to pose with a citizen who, at that time, was unknown to the public. Only much later did Boucher gain his present notoriety.

A task force made up of members of the Sûreté du Québec, the RCMP, and the Montreal police was formed specifically to deal with the bikers. At the end of summer 2000, members of this force – the Wolverine squad – had for months been following, recording, and establishing a series of facts that would allow them to build a major and unprecedented case against biker gang leaders. Police knew at the time that the Hells Angels had drawn up a blacklist of their enemies. Many individuals whose names were on that list were murdered. All of them had one thing in common: they were adversaries of the Hells Angels. Some were drug traffickers, others weren't.

The Hells Angels had also drawn up another list of people to be killed. This top-secret list included the names of several individuals with no direct link to the biker war. My name was apparently the first one on that list. The name of journalist Jocelyne Cazin, host of the popular program *JE* on the TVA network until 2001, was also on that list, as was that of Jacques Duchesneau, former director of the MUC police department. The bikers had also included the name of at least one cabinet member, that of Serge Ménard, Quebec's public security minister.

Even if plans to murder well-known people were dropped following the September 13 attempt, the gang went back to eliminating its enemies following a respite that lasted several weeks. Things started happening in a great rush after I was shot. The Hells Angels found themselves in a very bad position in criminal circles. Certain Mafia godfathers then gave orders. Peace absolutely had to be secured.

So, on September 26, leaders of the two rival biker gangs, the Hells Angels and Rock Machine, met in a room inside the Quebec City courthouse to start peace negotiations. Maurice Boucher and Fred Faucher had no trouble finding the way to the courthouse, since lawyers accompanied them.

On October 8, a peace agreement was signed and made official with a series of photographs later published in *Allô-Police*. Enemies had become friends. Because of this meeting, some journalists may become witnesses at Hells Angels' murder trials. The Crown may call upon them to attest that the photographed individuals have power, merely by shaking hands and embracing, to stop a series of more than sixty murders.

In January, the Wolverine squad caught all participants at the Table of Nine's weekly meeting. Detectives discovered on the premises photos of several Bandidos gang members targeted by new murder plots. To their great surprise, they also found pagers copied from the instruments belonging to enemies of the Angels. The conspirators were able to obtain information received by their enemies' pagers at the same time they did. Clones of the pagers used by police investigating the bikers were also found on members of the Hells Angels.

After March 2001, in the wake of the launch of Operation Spring 2001, Wolverine squad investigators obtained a great deal of information on the hidden side of this wretched war. Investigators also found out how certain bikers thought they were a special class within our society.

Two informers who started talking in the spring confirmed to Wolverine squad officers that the Hells Angels were linked to the September 13, 2000, murder attempt. Stéphane Faucher, called le Blond, and Serge Boutin, known as Pacha, made numerous revelations. One of them disclosed that, in the hours that followed the attempt, orders were given to the Rockers, the Hells Angels' underlings, to immediately stop all activities related to the list of those to be killed. The biker informers told police that an old member of the Rockers, Normand Bélanger, nicknamed la Pluche, is the one who disclosed orders from the Table of Nine.

Boutin also told investigators about circumstances surrounding the participation of René Charlebois, the newlywed, in the murder of Claude De Serres, a police informer, who was wearing a hidden microphone when he was killed near Notre-Dame-de-la-Merci, in the Laudière region. The Angels discovered his treachery when they read the files contained in the laptop computer belonging to an Ontario Provincial Police officer. The computer was stolen from the officer's hotel room in Sherbrooke when the police were engaged in a surveillance operation, watching an Angels' gathering. There's no doubt that the discovery that there were informers among them worried the bikers and led them to take drastic action later.

At least one Table of Nine leader is said to have gotten a larger share than the others of revenues from the gang's businesses, which seems to have surprised and angered his friends. Apparently, mutual suspicion among the malefactors is working to the point that police are certain that one or many of the gang leaders are considering the advantages of spilling the beans.

Police operations have dealt a serious blow to the Hells Angels organization, especially with the seizure of millions of dollars in cash. The full extent of the damage done to the organization won't be really be known for a few months, when information on the transfer of dirty money to tax havens will be disclosed.

Police investigations have revealed that bikers devised a scheme to launder money from drug sales by buying and selling cars. Many Quebec car dealers may find themselves embarrassed because they have acted in irregular ways. Dealers aren't allowed to sell vehicles into the United States, but bikers got around that difficulty by using ordinary people to buy large fully equipped vehicles. Social assistance recipients and poor people paid cash for vehicles worth between $50,000 and $60,000, without problem. Now that the secret has been discovered, a manufacturer has called to order one of his distributors, located on Montreal's south shore.

One of the bikers detained since the spring raid has already said he'd sold $40 million worth of vehicles across the border this way, an achievement that might well make honest business people jealous.

Though certain goods can easily be confiscated, others will surely escape the long arm of the law. Indeed, how could police seize the breast implants bikers gave their girlfriends who are topless dancers? These operations were paid for with drug money, but, like some other illicit profits, are surely beyond recovery now.

| 14 |

An Active Investigation

A few days after I came out of intensive care, investigators with the homicide squad inquired whether I could see them. Since they were looking for my aggressors, I obviously had things to tell them. "Our victims aren't usually very talkative," said Guy Bessette. It was clear that he and his colleague, Michel Whissel, had done their work. Since the attempt, they'd gathered more than a hundred pieces of information from the public, police circles, and several informers.

My visitors wanted to know if I had done any business over the last few months with the Société d'assurance automobile du Québec (SAAQ)*. I told them that I'd gone over to a SAAQ office to renew my driver's licence, but that I'd carried out no other transaction. They also asked whether I had dealt with the Ontario Street office, which is near my workplace. Again, I said no. I learned through their questions that personal information from my file had been obtained by a woman who worked at that office.

---

* The Quebec automobile insurance commission.

The detectives informed me that they had to carry on with their research, since it appeared the same person had examined the personal files of many of the other people who, like me, had been wounded or killed.

Later, I learned that people linked to the Hells Angels would pay $200 to obtain information from the SAAQ's confidential files.

The officers didn't say too much about their investigation, but I learned they had first-hand information on people linked to the automobile circle and on others linked to loan sharking for the Angels. In fact, I'd mentioned loan-sharking activities in my last article before the attempt. This was perhaps only a coincidence. Detectives gradually began to thoroughly check out the SAAQ lead. Later, they and I were surprised to see a member of the official Opposition in Quebec City disclose the existence of a mole who'd taken an interest in me.

Several months of research through SAAQ computer files were required to check all possible and imaginable leads before charges could be laid against the information officer suspected of examining my file. Over several months, investigators gathered an extensive file at the request of Randall Richmond, a lawyer with the Department of Justice's section for prosecuting organized crime. This meticulous lawyer handled the entire file on the attempt perpetrated against me. The prosecutor requested verifications that required countless hours of research. This research confirmed that organized criminals had managed to obtain everything they wanted from the SAAQ's confidential files. Police became disillusioned, since they'd previously believed that their information, as well as that related to bureaucrats and judges, was confidential. Criminals could obtain everything by simply asking for it with a fistful of dollars.

Those whose personal files were examined by the bikers were mostly enemies of the Hells Angels. Thirty-odd files referred to Rock Machine members, who officially became Bandidos in

2000, and drug dealers associated to the Dark Circle group, or simply minor traffickers the Angels wanted to eliminate.

One of the individuals targeted was Serge Bruneau, an opponent of Angels' expansion. The killers who went looking for him committed an enormous blunder. On August 26, 1999, a man showed up at Bruneau's business in Saint-Léonard and asked the individual there whether his name was Serge. The man said yes and the intruder pulled out a gun and shot him. Police who arrived on the murder scene only needed a few moments to understand the mistake. The victim was Serge Hervieux, a man who had nothing to do with the biker war. He earned an honest living working at this car and truck rental business. The man the bikers wanted to kill was his boss, who had the same first name.

The Hells Angels also obtained useful information from SAAQ files on the man who became their main opponent, Alain Brunette, the Bandidos' new president. Obtaining Brunette's addresses from the SAAQ, Angels killers went hunting. Since they couldn't find Brunette, his brother-in-law is the one who got it. Gilles Lesage was kidnapped while heading to a restaurant in Saint-Léonard. Police discovered that Lesage had been beaten before he was killed, which led investigators to believe he was interrogated.

On February 13, 2001, Brunette's pursuers caught up with him. As he was leaving a Sainte-Anne-des-Lacs residence in the Laurentians, he noticed he was being followed. He drove off at high speed along the Laurentian Highway to escape a barrage of gunfire. Several bullets went through his car, one of which struck him in the abdomen. He's still alive only because he turned around in the middle of traffic and drove at high speed in the opposite direction for nearly a kilometre along the fast lane. His passenger wasn't hit by the bullets.

Killers did intensive research on members of the Dark Circle, an independent gang that has resisted the Hells Angels' expansion. Many of these characters have been killed since 1995. But one member of that gang has always had incredible luck. Jean-Jacques Roy was the victim of two attempted murders. In November 1998, police saved his life by arresting two Angels associates who'd laid all the groundwork to kill him. Roy, as usual, refused to tell police a thing. He even declined to testify against his potential aggressors, which earned him a $2,500 fine for contempt of court.

Another member of the Dark Circle had his SAAQ file checked out. His name was Salvatore Brunetti. Killers never got to him, but he settled his problems with the Hells Angels by joining them. This switching of sides didn't benefit him since Brunetti was a victim of the anti-gang law in the huge March 2001 police raid against the Hells Angels. He was jailed for the murder of thirteen people, including many of his former associates, along with forty-one other Hells Angels members and leaders.

Altogether, moles at the SAAQ went through the files of three individuals who were later assassinated and of six people wounded with bullets during attempted murders. Three other people whose files were examined were also murdered, but it wasn't established whether confidential information is what helped killers find them.

On May 30, 2001, Ginette Martineau, forty-nine years of age, was arrested. This woman worked for an office affiliated with the SAAQ on Ontario Street. Her spouse, Raymond Turgeon, fifty-five years old, was also arrested. He allegedly relayed file details required by members of the Rockers, the Hells Angels' hired guns who operate mostly in Montreal. The couple is charged with fifty counts of illegally using a computer and breaches of trust. They're liable to ten-year prison sentences. The case is expected to go to trial in the summer of 2002.

Det.-Sgt. Guy Bessette discovered the SAAQ lead in the first hours of the investigation. But another lead was revealed shortly thereafter when the exhibits found at the crime scene were sent to the criminal science and legal medicine lab on Parthenais Street. Only a few hours were needed to confirm that two of the bullets removed from my body were fired from the weapon found shortly after the attempt. The ballistics expert recognized the pistol as being in every way similar to weapons he'd examined two years previously. That's how police were put on the trail of Michel Vézina, a Saint-Charles-sur-Richelieu resident.

Vézina is a perfectionist. He makes his own parts for improving the weapons he customizes. This is what led to his being identified as the maker of certain weapons submitted for expert analysis. He's passionate about firearms and is a skilful craftsman recognized in criminal circles for the effectiveness of his products. He has devoted his life to firearms.

When they first visited me in the hospital, the two investigators asked whether I knew him. I sifted through my memory, but that name didn't ring a bell. According to Bessette, I'd once written about this character. A phone call to the paper's archives confirmed that I had indeed written two articles on him in April 1998. My memory was quickly refreshed when I reread the articles. He was the Hells Angels' gunsmith. I had written that Vézina had for many years been the main supplier of machine guns, pistols, and silencers used by some of the killers involved in the war between rival gangs.

The Cobray machine gun, whose parts were purchased in the United States, was assembled here. Though the silencers were manufactured domestically, they were, according to RCMP gunsmiths, of a very high quality. By following the trail of a counterfeit network, police found the gunsmith network.

At the time, Vézina would sell a machine gun equipped with a silencer for $3,500. He'd also sell .22-calibre Ruger Mark II pistols equipped with silencers for $2,500. This is the preferred weapon of many killers. The bullets are smaller than those from machine guns, but their high velocity can cause a great deal of damage inside the victim's body. This type of weapon usually inflicts mortal wounds. Since the beginning of the 1990s, at least twenty murders and eleven attempted murders have been committed with similar weapons in Quebec. Vézina the gunsmith was once wounded by one of his own weapons. He accidentally shot himself through the hand with a volley of bullets when he was repairing a machine gun.

The RCMP discovered Vézina accidentally while investigating Laval criminals. An informer known exclusively by code number C-3409 provided enough information to put Const. Michel Lareau on Vézina's trail.

He was arrested on April 1, 1998. I was present with my colleague Pablo Durant when he and other prisoners were being led to RCMP cells in Westmount. While Durant was trying to photograph Vézina, I asked him a few questions, but he didn't answer, being rather busy hiding his face.

He denied his guilt at first, but Vézina then decided to admit everything. He was sentenced to thirty-four months in prison, and served eighteen of them before he was released. Following this release, he apparently went back to building weapons.

Investigators knew that Vézina had often travelled to Europe. He apparently made some fifteen trips to the region of Toulouse and Marseille in France, for unknown reasons. Police considered Vézina to be an accredited supplier to the Hells Angels, in Canada as well as Europe. However, he was never accused of trafficking weapons outside the country.

I saw Vézina one more time at his preliminary hearing at the Saint-Hyacinthe courthouse. I was called as a witness before Judge Gérard Girouard of the Quebec Court, who was to decide if evidence presented by the Crown prosecutor was sufficient to justify a trial. As the victim of a firearm injury, I was asked to briefly describe what had happened to me on September 13. I was questioned about my health and the after-effects of this attempted murder. In the few seconds Vézina and I exchanged glances, I thought I detected a certain embarrassment on his part, as though he wanted to apologize.

Vézina pleaded guilty and was sentenced to sixty-three months in jail by Judge Carol Saint-Cyr of the Quebec court.

While I was still in hospital, the police and my employers were beginning to discuss the possibility of offering a large reward to loosen tongues. In this kind of business, there are always people who know something about the identity of the criminals, their motives, or their associates. Many can be encouraged by the prospect of a reward to reveal their secrets. *Journal de Montréal* management provided $55,000 to investigators, who also obtained $20,000 from Jeunesse au Soleil. A generous donor from this charitable organization often makes large sums available to police to shed light on complex files.

However, in my case, this reward offer yielded no immediate results, at least not as far as I know. Nonetheless, detectives did get certain underworld secrets thanks to one of their informers. At the beginning of the investigation, this unknown character made disclosures that, at first, seemed totally ludicrous. Investigators and their bosses classify all information obtained according to a code designating its value. For instance, the opinion of a fortuneteller will be given less prominence than information from well-known informers or experienced police officers.

It took a few days for Bessette and Whissel to assess the information provided by the talkative informer. Obviously, according to what he was saying, the man was well placed within his circle. He knew several important people. However, what he was saying was so improbable that detectives decided to put him through a lie-detector test. Somewhat to the surprise of many people, the garrulous witness was telling the truth. He provided the name of the man who shot me. Bessette was having trouble believing what was happening. The investigation was taking a whole new turn.

The suspect was tailed, but proof of his participation in the attempt to kill me is far from being established. However, thanks to the tip, detectives have been on the trail of his accomplices and activities. An examination of this individual's communications allowed for the identification of at least three of his associates in the plot against me.

Thanks to their patience and to the use of technical and computer resources, investigators discovered proof that all the suspects had been in the area of the *Journal de Montréal* parking lot on the morning of the attempt, as well as on previous days. They also established that, twenty-three minutes following the attempt, the gunman turned up in a Saint-Catherine Street restaurant, near Papineau Avenue, where bikers with the Nomads chapter of the Hells Angels were already under police surveillance. Maurice Boucher was among the customers at the Club Sandwich restaurant, which was being watched by a special team of the Wolverine squad.

An hour later, all of the Nomads' top management was heading to another well-known downtown restaurant for a celebration. The Latini, a large Italian restaurant at the intersection of Jeanne-Mance Street and René-Lévesque Boulevard, had opened specifically for the Hells Angels at their request. Police officers observed the comings and goings of the bikers, as well as the precautions taken by their leaders to ensure they wouldn't be bothered. Biker employees opened the restaurant doors, allowing only invited guests to enter.

That day, the Nomads were holding their weekly "mass," the meeting where the club makes major and minor decisions. Police were apparently unable to find out what the gang was talking about. The bikers whispered into each other's ears and so avoided being heard by police microphones. Still, the investigation continues.

By Way of Conclusion

A t the beginning of summer 2001, the police had exhausted many of the leads they had followed in an effort to arrest the ten-odd people directly linked to the attempt on my life. Obtaining information and identifying suspects is the easiest part of a police investigation. Getting evidence is more difficult. Chief André Bouchard, of the MUC police's major crimes division, often repeats that only a little more evidence is needed to charge all those involved in the plot to kill me. He revealed that technical evidence had already established the genetic profile of one conspirator. "The killer has been identified," he said.

For my part, I went back to life as usual, convinced that those responsible for the attempt, having failed the first time, were unlikely to try again. Some of the information obtained suggests they understood the futility of their action and that one less journalist wouldn't change a thing to coverage of the biker war. They understood that the failed attempt had led politicians to pass harsher laws and police to follow their illicit activities more closely.

I'm more than ever convinced that firearms are a danger to society. Hunters can have access to their weapons, but the ownership and use of handguns, automatic and semi-automatic weapons must be made more difficult.

During my visit to the Mexican countryside last January, I caught myself jumping when I heard gunshots in the village where I was staying. The sounds were muffled, exactly like those from the weapon of the man who shot me in the *Journal de Montréal* parking lot. That's just about the only time in the last several months that I vividly remembered the attempt.

I have had a lot of time to think about my feelings towards the conspirators and the gunman. Try as I might to find a trace of vengeance deep within me, I can't do it. I believe that the police will manage to arrest them some day. It often happens that a new informer will, several months after a crime, unveil information useful to police in bringing criminals before a judge. That's probably what will happen with the investigation on the attempt to kill me. In any event, it's very likely that the guilty parties will be arrested for other crimes. These conspirators are crooks who are very active in their field and some are in custody already.

Police summoned me to the homicide squad's offices to show me the video taken by the surveillance camera. Although they said nothing about the goal of this exercise, I immediately understood that the individual who appeared on screen was the one who had tried to kill me September 13, 2000. But seeing that face awakened no memory. I was unable to identify other people on a second surveillance cassette.

I thought that sight of the killer's face would kindle my emotions, but I remained unmoved. Never did I feel any fear either.

Many people praised my courage, my strength of character, and my determination. I was congratulated for the example I can give to people facing hardship. But I personally don't understand why I managed to survive this attempted murder. Why bullets that passed centimetres – what am I saying? millimetres – from vital organs didn't leave me paralyzed or dead.

Perhaps I still have things to accomplish on this earth.

Acknowledgements

I wrote this book while often thinking about my friends Jeannine Bourdages and Claude Masson, who died in the October 1999 crash of EgyptAir Flight 990. Why did they die and why am I still alive? Who decides our destiny?

It's impossible here to thank all the people who helped me in my personal and professional lives. I should also thank all the unknown individuals who encouraged or congratulated me following the attempt. I can't do so personally so I convey a general and sincere thank you to them here.

On the professional side, I have to highlight the exceptional contribution of past and present journalistic colleagues. Thanks to Jacques Ébacher, Raymond Drouin, Marcel Lamarche, François Béliveau, François Trépanier. Thanks to Rodolphe Morissette, the best crime reporter I know and an important source of inspiration.

Thanks to the entire team of photographers with the *Journal de Montréal*. A special thank you as well to a team of ladies who always work in the shadows but who are important allies to a journalist: the archivists and phone operators. Thanks to Lucie

218

The Biker Who Shot Me

Sansregret, Sylvie Mayer, Céline Raymond, Monique Houle, Aline Dupuis, and Catherine Martel.

I'll forever be grateful to the people at Urgences-Santé and to the McGill University Medical Centre team, headed by surgeon David Evans.

This book would have never been possible without the efforts of Pierre Turgeon, Hélène Noël, and Louis Royer from Trait d'union publishing. For the translation of the book, thank you to Jean-Paul Murray and to Jonathan Webb, my editor at McClelland & Stewart.

A last thank you to my fellow journalists in Montreal and Toronto, who are both friends and competitors: James Dubro, Peter Edwards, Peter Moon, Adrian Humphreys, Antonio Nicaso, Lee Lamothe, Jack Boland, Rob Lamberti, Marcel Laroche, and André Cédilot.